At *Issue

Protecting America's Borders

Douglass Stinson, *Book Editor*

Bruce Glassman, *Vice President*
Bonnie Szumski, *Publisher*
Helen Cothran, *Managing Editor*

GREENHAVEN PRESS
An imprint of Thomson Gale, a part of The Thomson Corporation

THOMSON
*
GALE

Detroit • New York • San Francisco • San Diego • New Haven, Conn.
Waterville, Maine • London • Munich

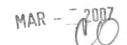

For more information, contact
Greenhaven Press
27500 Drake Rd.
Farmington Hills, MI 48331-3535
Or you can visit our Internet site at http://www.gale.com

LIBRARY OF CONGRESS CATALOGING-IN-PUBLICATION DATA

Protecting America's borders / Douglass Stinson, book editor.
    p. cm. — (At issue)
Includes bibliographical references and index.
ISBN 0-7377-2739-X (lib. : alk. paper) — ISBN 0-7377-2740-3 (pbk. : alk. paper)
    1. United States—Emigration and immigration—Government policy. 2. Visas—Government policy—United States. 3. Terrorism—United States—Prevention. 4. National security—United States. I. Stinson, Douglass. II. At issue (San Diego, Calif.)
JV6483.P76 2005
363.28'5'0973—dc22   2004060857

Printed in the United States of America

Contents

Introduction

On June 18, 2001, Congressional Research Service analysts William Krouse and Raphael Perl submitted a report to members of Congress arguing that strengthening U.S. borders against international terrorists was vital to national security. The authors pinpointed weaknesses in border controls and urged congressional support of measures aimed at

> (1) making it more difficult to counterfeit and alter international travel documents, (2) increasing entry/exit control mechanisms at international ports of entry, (3) increasing staff and technology for consular and federal inspection services, (4) enhancing record-keeping on the visa status and whereabouts of foreign students in the United States, and (5) expanding the current visa lookout system to include data on members of international organized crime groups.

The report generated little publicity. Then, only twelve weeks later, terrorists who had exploited the weaknesses addressed by Krouse and Perl successfully attacked New York City and Washington, D.C., and the issue of protecting America's borders catapulted to the forefront of public and legislative debate. Law enforcement, intelligence-gathering, and border protection agencies suddenly faced demands for stricter controls on immigration and visa issuance, improved port and cargo inspection, and better monitoring of the activities of potentially subversive organizations. A shocked nation debated how to divide responsibilities among federal, state, and local governments; how to fund and staff new programs; and how to increase surveillance and reporting requirements without violating constitutional guarantees of privacy and individual rights. Existing controls had proved inadequate; the question now was how to screen the traffic of goods and people crossing U.S. borders to identify possible terrorists and keep them out.

The result has been the most significant government reorganization since the creation of the Department of Defense in

1947. Understanding the debate over how best to protect America's borders and strengthen national security depends on basic familiarity with a bewildering array of new agencies and far-reaching programs, beginning with deciphering their acronyms and defining their overlapping purposes.

In March 2003 the Department of Homeland Security (DHS) officially began operation as a new executive branch cabinet department responsible for preventing, protecting against, and responding to threats to the nation such as terrorist attacks and other emergencies. The DHS was divided into four directorates: The Border and Transportation Security (BTS) directorate is the one most directly responsible for protecting and strengthening America's borders. A number of well-known agencies, including the U.S. Customs Service (formerly in the Treasury Department), the Immigration and Naturalization Service, and the U.S. Border Patrol (formerly in the Justice Department), were brought under the BTS roof and reorganized as three new entities.

The Bureau of Citizenship and Immigration Services (CIS or USCIS) is a primarily administrative agency with about ten thousand employees. It processes applications for visas, residency green cards, naturalization, and citizenship; adjudicates asylum and refugee claims; and issues and renews immigration documents and benefits.

U.S. Immigration and Customs Enforcement (ICE) has both investigative and enforcement responsibilities. Its fifteen thousand employees are charged with investigating threats to national security and enforcing immigration and customs laws within the country. Thus, the ICE operates forensic laboratories to detect and counter forged immigration documents; apprehends and deports immigration violators; and investigates smugglers, international arms dealers, and money launderers as well as potential terrorists. The ICE also maintains extensive, searchable immigration databases of individuals' entrance and exit history, record of criminal convictions and other personal information, and current visa status.

U.S. Customs and Border Protection (CPB), with a staff of forty-one thousand, is the BTS bureau most closely associated with manning the nation's actual borders. Its task is enormous. On a typical day, the CPB reports, the agency

- processes more than 1.1 million passengers and pedestrians, including 724,192 aliens; 64,432 truck, rail, and sea containers; 2,639 aircraft; 365,079 vehicles;

- executes more than 135 arrests at ports of entry; 3,179 arrests between ports of entry;
- seizes an average of 2,313 pounds of narcotics in 131 narcotic seizures at ports of entry; $205,576 in currency; 193 firearms; $1.9 million in merchandise at ports of entry; 49 vehicles;
- refuses entry of 1,237 noncitizens at ports of entry; 54 criminal aliens attempting to enter the United States;
- intercepts more than 210 fraudulent documents; 1 traveler for terrorism/national security concerns; 1 stowaway;
- protects more than 5,000 miles of border with Canada; 1,900 miles of border with Mexico.

The CIS, ICE, and CPB have not worked together smoothly under the new organization. In 2004, budget crises, turf disputes, and the difficulties of implementing a number of ambitious programs led lawmakers to request audits and investigations of possible financial and operational mismanagement. Despite new antiterrorism demands, the department announced hiring and spending freezes and quietly released more than sixteen hundred detainees from facilities in the United States to cut costs. In March 2005 new homeland security chief Michael Chertoff announced plans to review the policies and structure of the BTS, and critics of the Bush administration's handling of border protection issues have advanced several proposals, from merging ICE and CBP to taking control of some homeland security programs out of federal hands entirely. Meanwhile, debate focuses on the value, constitutionality, and effectiveness of some key homeland security initiatives.

The new programs fall into two groups: those that affect people crossing U.S. borders and those that affect goods crossing U.S. borders.

One early post–September 11 program, the National Security Entry-Exit Registration System, or NSEERS, drew heavy criticism as an example of government-sponsored discrimination. Conducted by the CIS, beginning in September 2002 NSEERS required adult male foreign visitors from twenty-five predominantly Arab and Muslim countries to report to immigration authorities for so-called special registration (which included fingerprinting) when they entered the United States and again thirty days later. Thousands who voluntarily reported for registration were detained or deported, leading many others to flee to Canada, and some twenty to eighty men reportedly remain in custody. Public charges that NSEERS discriminatorily violated law-abiding citizens' civil rights led to the cancellation of several disputed provisions in December 2003, and the program was replaced in January 2004 by the U.S. Visitor and Immigrant Status Indicator Technology (US-VISIT) program, which requires all visa-holding visitors to the United States to be photographed and finger-scanned at entry and exit points without regard to national origin, religion, or sex.

One of the most far-reaching new programs, the Container and Security Initiative (CSI) involves the importation and transport of goods into the United States. CSI is a joint venture between the U.S. government (specifically, the CBP) and twenty countries around the world that are home to ports that ship the greatest volume of containers—by which 90 percent of the world's cargo is moved today—to the United States. Participating countries agree to allow CBP teams to establish offices in the home ports, to deliver cargo manifests to the U.S. agents twenty-four hours before containers leave the port, and to inspect all containers bound for the United States that are identified as potential threats. The CBP promotes CSI as beneficial to the host countries because their prescreened containers will get expedited processing when they are off-loaded onto U.S. piers (essentially making them preferred trading partners), and because, in the event of a terrorist attack using a cargo container, the United States would most likely halt shipping from non-CSI ports, giving CSI ports a competitive advantage.

These are some of the new border protection tools being used in the war on terrorism. The contributors to *At Issue: Protecting America's Borders* debate their effectiveness and discuss their effects on Americans' lives since September 11. That day marks the beginning of a new awareness of America's vulnerability, and of intense efforts to make the nation safer.

1

Federal Immigration Controls Fail to Protect America's Borders

Steven A. Camarota

Steven A. Camarota is director of research at the Center for Immigration Studies, a nonprofit, nonpartisan research organization based in Washington, D.C.

America's immigration controls are negligible, allowing terrorists and enemies of the United States to enter the country at will. Foreign visa applicants should be treated as potential suspects, rather than visitors, until they are proven to be harmless. Immigration procedures must be overhauled, starting with removing State Department diplomats from the visa-issuing process. Tougher screening and ID checks for travelers at ports of entry are necessary to catch terrorists before they strike. An overwhelming majority of Americans of all races and backgrounds supports strict immigration measures, even if such actions make international travel inconvenient.

All 19 perpetrators of the horrific attacks of September 11 [2001] were foreign citizens who had entered the United States as students, business travelers, or tourists. Clearly, changes in our immigration procedures, including temporary and permanent visa issuance, border control, and efforts to deal with illegal immigration, are critical to reducing the chances of further attacks. In the new kind of war we now face, the primary weapons are the terrorists themselves, so keeping them out or

Steven A. Camarota, "Tighten America's Borders," *The American Enterprise*, December 2001, pp. 42–45. Copyright © 2001 by *The American Enterprise*, a magazine of Politics, Business, and Culture. On the web at www.TAEmag.com. Reproduced by permission.

apprehending them after they get in is going to be an indispensable element of victory. The simple fact is that if the terrorists can't enter the country, they won't be able to commit a terror attack on American soil.

> *If the terrorists can't enter the country, they won't be able to commit a terror attack on American soil.*

Most Americans understand that our border is a critical tool for protecting America's national interests. A Zogby poll taken in the wake of the attacks found that the overwhelming majority of Americans, across all races, regions, incomes, and political beliefs, blamed lax border control and screening of immigrants for contributing to the attacks. There can be little doubt that greatly stepped-up efforts to control the border would be met with overwhelming support by the American people. Unfortunately a small but influential portion of America's leadership has come to see borders as simply an obstacle to be overcome by travelers and businesses. This attitude has to change.

Entry to the United States is not a right but a privilege, granted exclusively at our discretion. For the most part that discretion is exercised by members of the State Department's Bureau of Consular Affairs, often referred to as the Consular Corps. Among their other duties, these men and women make the all-important decisions about who gets a visa to enter the United States, making them the forward guard of homeland defense—America's other Border Patrol. Unfortunately, the Consular Corps badly needs more manpower and improved tools in order to fulfill these responsibilities properly.

Tough Visa Screening

Some changed procedures and attitudes are also required. It must be reasserted that the American people, and not visa applicants, are the customer. The Consular Corps has adopted a culture of service rather than skepticism, in which visa officers feel it is as important to please visa applicants as it is to screen them thoroughly. There has been pressure to speed processing and to approve marginal applications.

Responsibility for issuing visas fell to the State Department because it was the only agency with offices overseas, where the demand was. But it is difficult to imagine two less complementary functions than diplomacy and enforcement of immigration laws. The diplomat's goal of promoting cooperation and compromise is sometimes in conflict with the gatekeeper's goal of exposing fraud and ensuring compliance with the law. This systemic mismatch is likely to persist regardless of management changes and may only be remedied by transferring all visa-issuing responsibilities overseas to the U.S. Immigration and Naturalization Service [INS], or perhaps a new "Visa Corps" answerable to the U.S. head of Homeland Security. Visa officers need to be highly trained professionals, specializing in their function, respected by their agency, and insulated from political pressure.

Administrative changes won't matter much, of course, if there aren't enough people to handle the work. The current Bureau of Consular Affairs has only 900 officers overseas, assisted by 2,500 foreign nationals, yet the demand for visas to visit the United States is enormous. Last year, the State Department issued 7.1 million non-immigrant visas, more than triple the number issued 30 years ago. So consular officers often have no more than a few minutes to assess each application.

> *It is difficult to imagine two less complementary functions than diplomacy and enforcement of immigration laws.*

Because of this ballooning workload, all junior Foreign Service officers are required to adjudicate visa applications for a year or more. That has turned this profound responsibility into a dreaded rite of passage for new Foreign Service officers, and visa responsibilities are held in low regard institutionally.

We also need tougher standards. For instance, visa officers should be instructed to deny entry permits to people who are clearly enemies of America, even if they haven't actually committed a terrorist act. Currently, the law makes it extremely difficult to turn down an applicant because of his "beliefs, statements, or associations, if such beliefs, statements, or associations would be lawful within the United States." At present, keeping out someone who distributes Osama bin Laden videos, or even a terrorist sympathizer who publicly organizes demonstrations calling for the destruction of America, requires the secretary of state to personally make the decision and then report the case to Congress. As a result, few if any individuals are excluded based on their anti-American beliefs.

"Watch List" Based on Country of Origin

Individuals expressing strong anti-American views should be added to the "watch list" used to deny visas. Some may object to the idea of excluding people based on their political beliefs, but being denied a visa does not prevent a person from expressing his views, it simply prevents him from living in this country.

Additionally, citizens of countries with many terrorism or terrorist sympathizers (Egypt and Saudi Arabia, for example) should have to pass a much higher bar for visa issuance, including a thorough security clearance (working with local authorities). No visas should be issued to citizens of Middle Eastern countries at U.S. consulates outside their home countries—an American visa officer in Germany is less likely to be able to identify a problem applicant from Saudi Arabia than his counterpart based in Saudi Arabia. There is nothing unusual about country-specific variations in visa policies. A citizen of Poland currently needs a visa to vacation in the United States, while a Japanese national does not.

The next layer of protection is the border itself, which has two elements: 1) ports of entry where travelers enter the United States, and 2) the stretches between those entry points. The first are staffed by immigration and Customs inspectors, the second, are monitored by the Border Patrol and the Coast Guard.

> *Individuals expressing strong anti-American views should be added to the 'watch list' used to deny visas.*

We need a greater investment of manpower and infrastructure at each of these levels—many more inspectors and more inspection lanes at crossing points. Immigrant smuggling was almost completely shut down when security was tightened after the September 11 attacks. Continuing this more intensive checking, using additional inspectors to avoid excessive delays, can yield much better security.

We should have learned our lesson in December 1999, when Ahmed Ressam was stopped by a border inspector in Washington state. He had trained at bin Laden's terrorist camps in Afghanistan and had a car full of explosives with which he was going to disrupt millennium celebrations in Seattle and blow up Los Angeles International Airport. He had entered Canada with a forged passport, requested political asylum, and been released into the Canadian population.

Track Foreigner Entries and Exits

As part of improved border control we need an accurate system for tracking the U.S. entries and exits of foreigners. There is currently no mechanism for tracking land departures, and the system for tracking arrivals and departures by air is completely broken. We have no way of knowing whether foreign visitors admitted on visas actually leave the country when their visas expire. There are an estimated 3 to 4 million people living in the United States who entered the country legally but never left, accounting for perhaps 40 percent of the total illegal-alien population, but we have no way of picking them out.

> *The system for tracking arrivals and departures by air is completely broken.*

In 1994, the bipartisan U.S. Commission on Immigration Reform, headed by the late Barbara Jordan, called for computerized tracking of all arrivals and departures by land, sea, and air (including Canadians, who don't need visas). In the 1996 immigration law, Congress directed the INS to develop such a system, but this provision was postponed and in 2000 effectively shelved, partly at the behest of businesses in border states. The concern was that the system would create interminable traffic jams. A technologically modern system with an adequate number of scanners should not significantly impede traffic at all, however. This, of course, would require greatly increased investment in equipment and personnel at our borders.

A tightly monitored entry-exit system would be of limited value if it continues to be easy to cross our borders illegally. A serious attempt has been made in recent years to expand the Border Patrol, although the total number of agents is still only about 9,000. It may be a reasonable long-term goal to triple that number. Recent patrol improvements along our Mexican border, which have reduced illegal crossings, need to be extended and transferred to the Canadian border as well—where terrorists, for a variety of reasons, are more likely to cross.

Restrict Student Visas

So long as we continue to neglect enforcement of immigration law and allow millions of illegals to live in our country, we will expose our country to very significant terrorist threats. Fortunately there are a number of steps we can take.

Tracking foreign residents granted admission to the U.S. for extended periods is quite possible with the assistance of the American institution responsible for their whereabouts. At least one of the September 11 terrorists entered the country on a student visa, yet never showed up for a class, without triggering any concern anywhere. This should not be possible.

The 1996 immigration law mandated that the INS develop a computerized tracking system for foreign students, to replace the current paper-based, manual system. Unfortunately, the system has not gone beyond the pilot stage, and is only being tested in a couple of dozen southeastern schools, largely because of opposition from colleges.

> We know Middle East terrorists (and other unwanted visitors) now routinely enter this country using aliases and forged identity documents—as several of the September 11 hijackers did.

The nature of a visiting student's studies should also be a legitimate matter of concern. We currently make little or no effort to prevent students from terrorism-sponsoring states from studying subjects that could be used in weapons programs. A lack of monitoring allows students to declare their intention to study an innocuous social science, for instance, but then change to nuclear engineering or microbiology without anyone being alerted to this fact.

Visiting Privileges

The INS tracking system now in development should be expanded to cover foreigners working in the U.S. as well as students. Biometric identifiers like a fingerprint scanning system are critical, because we know Middle East terrorists (and other unwanted visitors) now routinely enter this country using aliases and forged identity documents—as several of the September 11 hijackers did. Biometric tracking of foreigners should be used at each border crossing, each change in school or work status, each arrest, each application for government benefits. This tracking file should be accessible to law enforcement authorities.

Civil libertarians may howl. But remember, these are not American citizens entitled to full American freedoms; they are guests from overseas whose presence here is a privilege. Americans will have to wait in longer lines and endure tighter checks from now on; it is not too much to ask foreign citizens to do the same. The simple truth is, there is no alternative to improved monitoring if we want to keep admitting large numbers of foreign citizens while protecting national security as well.

Some may object to increased screening, law enforcement, and border control on the grounds that only a fraction of all immigrants and visitors who come to the United States each year break laws or represent a threat. We are, some would say, looking for a needle in a haystack. But then all security measures are directed at small numbers of lawbreakers within large groups. Millions of people boarding airplanes must pass through metal detectors and have their baggage X-rayed in a search for needles in the haystack. It is the same with screening foreign visitors.

To be sure, no reforms will catch all those who mean us harm. But we can make enormous improvements. If only one of the people involved in the September 11 plot had been identified by a consular officer, or when he entered the United States, or when his visa expired, the entire conspiracy might have been uncovered. Only a well-funded and well-run immigration system will be able to put to use the new information that will result from improved intelligence gathering over coming years. The different elements in national security all interconnect. Today's antiquated system for controlling our borders is one of our weakest links.

2

America's New Border Protection Forces Are Improving National Security

Asa Hutchinson

Asa Hutchinson is the undersecretary in charge of the Department of Homeland Security's Border and Transportation Security directorate.

The reorganization of federal agencies responsible for protecting U.S. borders, ports, and transportation systems has already made the country safer due to better cooperation between agencies and more efficient operation. Automated visa tracking, electronic screening systems for baggage at airports, and other new technologies have been deployed to better thwart the entry of terrorists and weapons or materials that could harm Americans. Federal officers from U.S. Customs, the Immigration and Naturalization Service, and the Transportation Security Administration are working together like never before to ensure the homeland is more secure now and in the future.

S ecuring our nation's air, land, and sea borders is a difficult yet critical task. The United States has 5,525 miles of border with Canada and 1,989 miles with Mexico. Our maritime border includes 95,000 miles of shoreline, and a 3.4 million square mile exclusive economic zone. Each year, more than 500 million people cross the borders into the United States, some 330 million of

Asa Hutchinson, statement before the U.S. House Select Committee on Homeland Security, Washington, DC, June 25, 2003.

whom are non-citizens, through our 350 ports of entry.

The Border and Transportation Security [BTS] Directorate is one of five Directorates within DHS [Department of Homeland Security], and in partnership with the U.S. Coast Guard [USCG], watches over our nation's borders and transportation systems. The BTS Directorate is comprised of the former U.S. Customs Service, the Immigration and Naturalization Service, the Transportation Security Administration [TSA], the Office of Domestic Preparedness (ODP), the Inspections Division of the Agriculture Plant Health Inspections Service (APHIS), the Federal Protective Service (FPS), and the Federal Law Enforcement Training Center (FLETC). Its extraordinarily dedicated employees—over 100,000 of them—were brought together under the BTS roof because of their common focus of ensuring the security of our nation's borders, ports of entry and transportation systems, on facilitating the flow of legitimate commerce and on enforcing our nation's immigration laws. . . .

> *US-VISIT will make entry easier for legitimate travelers and more difficult for illegal entrants.*

Since the creation of the Department [in January 2003], . . . the BTS Directorate has taken a number of strides to integrate its component agencies and streamline their operations. We have achieved a number of operational and programmatic successes and challenges since the 24th of January [2003], and I'd like to share some of those accomplishments with you in the hope that you will share my assessment that we are indeed, off to good start.

Many Accomplishments

Since its inception on January 24, 2003, the Border and Transportation Security Directorate has:

• Initiated a comprehensive reorganization of its component agencies, creating two new bureaus: the Bureau of Immigration and Customs Enforcement [BICE], and the Bureau of Customs and Border Protection [BCBP].

• Deployed new technologies and tools at land, air and sea borders;

• Expedited distribution of billions of dollars in grant monies to states and cities, with more to come.

• Created a 24 hour Radiation/WMD [weapons of mass destruction] Hotline to assist BCBP and BICE officers with scientific and technical needs regarding Chemical, Biological, Radiological and Nuclear (CBRN) alerts along the border. . . .

• BTS is in the first phase of developing the US-VISIT system and we will have an initial deployment at air and sea ports of entry by December 31, 2003. The system will be capable of tracking the entry and exit of foreign visitors who require a visa to the U.S. US-VISIT will make entry easier for legitimate travelers and more difficult for illegal entrants through the use of biometrically authenticated documents. . . .

Safety in the Air

TSA's approach to transportation security is one designed to provide layered protection. To date, TSA has achieved significant accomplishments in both its overall approach and within the specific transportation modes:

• TSA is screening passengers and checked baggage at our nation's airports, including electronic explosives detection for checked baggage at nearly all commercial aviation airports—all within the congressionally mandated deadlines and all with the congressionally approved methods of screening set forth in the Aviation and Transportation Security Act that was passed by Congress and signed by President [George W.] Bush on Nov. 19, 2001. As a side note, I would like to mention that nationally, about 92 percent of all bags are screened electronically. Prior to 9/11 only about 5 percent of all bags were being screened by any means.

• TSA is working with airports on the installation of equipment needed to screen all bags electronically and is preparing Letters of Intent for several major airports that will commit federal funds to projects for the installation of electronic screening equipment.

Improved Screening

• TSA dramatically expanded the Federal Air Marshals program to cover a significant percentage of both international and domestic flights.

• TSA worked with the FAA [Federal Aviation Administration], in administering a program for air carriers to install hardened cockpit doors for commercial passenger aircraft.

• TSA is developing a new and improved successor to the current Computer Assisted Passenger Prescreening System (CAPPS). CAPPS II will assist the agency in identifying terrorist threats to the aviation system while also dramatically reducing the number of travelers subjected to additional screening procedures at the nation's airports. This system is being carefully designed to improve security while respecting the civil liberties of American travelers. . . .

> *Prior to 9/11, only about 5 percent of all bags were being screened by any means.*

• TSA launched Federal Flight Deck Officer training program to enable qualified flight crews to be armed while on duty. The first class concluded on April 19th, with 44 pilots certified to carry firearms in the cockpit as Federal Flight Deck Officers.

• TSA developed a strengthened "Known Shipper" program for air cargo including strengthened requirements to achieve Known Shipper status, and is developing additional layers of security to "pre-screen" cargo for targeted inspections.

• TSA has worked with airlines, airports and other airport employers to ensure that background checks have been done on all of their employees. This includes criminal background checks done by the airports. More than 1 million background checks have been completed. . . .

Better Inspections

• The Bureau of Customs and Border Protection has consolidated incoming inspectional resources into a single face of government at ports of entry by establishing Interim Port Directors to integrate all of the incoming border agencies into one chain of command. A single field manager can implement a change in threat level in what used to be three disparate workforces.

• BCBP continues to deploy multiple technologies to support our layered inspection process, using various technologies in different combinations to detect the adversary who might defeat a single sensor or device.

• To date, more than 180 devices that are non-intrusive inspection systems and/or portal radiation detection devices have been deployed to detect and deter the entry of radiological material into the country.

• BCBP has provided all of its front-line (BCBP) inspectors across the country with personal radiation detectors that alert them to the presence of radioactive material. . . .

More Agents

• BCBP continues to harden the entire Northern Border ports-of-entry through the installation of technology and infrastructure, such as barriers, gates, bollards, lighting and video security systems.

• The Border Patrol will deploy an additional 387 agents along the U.S. and Canadian border by January 2004, bringing the total number of agents deployed to over 1,000.

• BCBP's Border Patrol has deployed additional helicopters and fixed wing aircraft at 8 Northern Border Sectors and at 7 of the 9 Southern Border Sectors.

> *The FAST program enables the Bureau of Customs and Border Protection to focus its security efforts and inspections on high-risk commerce.*

• Integrated Border Enforcement Teams have been created in each Northern Border Sector to promote better coordination and inter-operability among law enforcement agencies and the Royal Canadian Mounted Police.

• In FY [fiscal year] 2003, the Border Patrol has removed 100,886 illegal aliens so far. This is in addition to the 149,067 removed in FY 2002.

• BCBP is implementing the Free and Secure Trade Initiative (FAST). The FAST program enables the Bureau of Customs and Border Protection to focus its security efforts and inspections on high-risk commerce while making sure legitimate, low-risk commerce faces no unnecessary and costly delays. NEXUS and SENTRI [programs that allow registered users to cross the border quickly] are also being implemented to facilitate the travel of legitimate visitors on the Northern and Southern Borders.

• BCBP continues implementation of the Customs-Trade Partnership Against Terrorism (C-TPAT), a public-private partnership aimed at securing the global supply chain against terrorism, while also facilitating legitimate trade.

• The Container Security Initiative [CSI] has established tough new procedures targeting high-risk cargo containers before they embark en-route to U.S. ports. 19 ports (including 3 Canadian)—through which approximately two-thirds of cargo containers coming to the U.S. will pass—have agreed to participate in the program. 10 initial ports are operational.

• Along with CSI, BCBP began enforcing the new 24-hour rule in February [2003], requiring submission of electronic advance cargo manifests by sea carriers 24 hours before U.S.-bound cargo is loaded aboard the vessel at a foreign port. The information obtained is used as a factor in determining which containers are high-risk. This foreign based activity can preclude a risk from ever arriving in the USA.

• BCBP continues to coordinate with the Coast Guard to have expanded Passenger Analysis Units at seaports around the country to target and identify high-risk travelers and immediately react to threats. BCBP cross checks advance notice of arrival information provided to the USCG 96-hours prior to arrival at U.S. ports, rather than the previous 24-hour notice, for potentially dangerous crew, passengers and cargo, thus allowing USCG to act appropriately prior to arrival in the U.S. port.

• BCBP requires all airlines to provide information on U.S.-bound passengers prior to their arrival; information is then checked against the FBI's and other relevant databases.

• BCBP's National Targeting Center and enhanced Automated Targeting System continue to identify those containers and travelers that pose a high risk of terrorism.

Immigration Changes

• BICE combined all the investigative functions of Customs, Immigration and the Federal Protective Service into one bureau. BICE has taken steps to provide a single point of contact within DHS for U.S. Attorneys and other law enforcement agencies.

• In conjunction with the Foreign Terrorist Tracking Task Force, BICE agents have apprehended more than 1,000 immigrants for a variety of offenses of which over 500 were deported.

• Operation Joint Venture, a special operation initiated by BICE to identify and remove persons with unknown or questionable identities with access to restricted areas of military installations, has resulted in 37 arrests, of which 28 were removed from the United States.

Bolster Enforcement

• BICE's Operation No Mercy, initiated after the tragic deaths of 19 persons believed to be undocumented aliens in Texas, has resulted in the indictment of 14 individuals.

• BICE acquired and deployed additional "A-STAR" and "HUEY" helicopters to bolster enforcement efforts along the U.S. Southern Border.

• BICE continues in its efforts to ensure the integrity and lawful operation of U.S. Financial systems.

• Project Shield America, a BICE initiative, continues to prevent sensitive U.S. technology and munitions from falling into the hands of terrorists and other U.S. adversaries. Under this initiative, BICE agents partner with U.S. manufacturers and exporters to guard against illegal arms exports. . . .

> *BCBP requires all airlines to provide information on U.S.-bound passengers prior to their arrival.*

This list is far from complete, but I believe it shows that the BTS Directorate is hard at work on the task before us. We are shaping a new department, improving the security of our country and still sustaining the centuries old traditions of operational excellence that our individual components have brought to the BTS Directorate.

Because of the efforts of the dedicated employees of the Border and Transportation Security Directorate, undertaken in partnership with the American people, our federal, state, local, private and international counterparts, and our other colleagues within the Department of Homeland Security, America is becoming safer and more secure every day. A number of challenges lie ahead, but we are taking the necessary steps to improve the security of our borders, ports of entry, transportation systems; facilitate the movements of people and goods.

3

Racial Profiling Increases Border Security

Richard Lowry

Richard Lowry is the editor of the National Review *and a syndicated columnist.*

In today's atmosphere of terrorism, race and nationality are valid predictors of whether individuals represent a terrorist threat. Since over half the FBI's most wanted terrorists are Arab, security officials should be profiling, or paying extra attention to, travelers with Arab backgrounds. To equate these security measures with civil rights violations is lazy thinking. Further, treating passengers equally as terrorist threats is expensive, causes delays, and wastes resources that could be better spent finding actual terrorists. Instead, the United States should look to Israel for examples of effective security measures that take into account individuals' backgrounds.

In late September [2001], M. Ahsan Baig was kept off United Flight 288 from San Francisco to Philadelphia because the pilot didn't like the way he seemed to be furtively talking to another passenger in the waiting area. Baig, a California computer specialist who is from Pakistan, got on another flight 90 minutes later after apologies from a ticket agent. An hour-and-a-half delay, for many fliers, might be considered a good day at the airport. For Baig, it was the occasion for a civil-rights lawsuit.

So it goes at the nation's airports. An Arab-American Secret Service agent's recent difficulty boarding a flight with his gun has become a national scandal. Meanwhile, discrimination

Richard Lowry, "Profiles in Cowardice: How to Deal with the Terrorist Threat and How Not To," *National Review*, vol. 54, January 28, 2002. Copyright © 2002 by the National Review, Inc., 215 Lexington Ave., New York, NY 10016. Reproduced by permission.

lawsuits filed by Arab-American men have become the latest cause. . . . September 11 may have changed the world, but grievance politics is one corner of it that has been serenely untouched. Arab-American groups still scream at any suggestion of commonsense security at airports, while the [George W.] Bush administration still cowers at any association with "racial profiling." It has become clear in recent weeks that the pieties of American racial politics will remain unchanged—even after contributing to a mass murder.

Arab Characteristics

No one likes to say it out loud, but more than half the people on the FBI's Most Wanted terrorist list are named Mohammed, Ahmed, or both (for instance, Ahmed Mohammed Hamed Ali). Islamic terrorists will necessarily be Muslims, and probably from the Arab world. Not to profile for those characteristics is simply to ignore the nature of today's terrorism. As security expert Neil Livingstone points out, when the [radical black nationalist group] Black Panthers were hijacking planes in the 1970s, security personnel should have been on the lookout for young black men; when D.B. Cooper—the famed skyjacker who parachuted out of a plane with a bagful of cash in 1971—was on the public mind, security should have been suspicious of young-to-middle-aged white men booked to fly over rugged terrain.

> *No one likes to say it out loud, but more than half the people on the FBI's Most Wanted terrorist list are named Mohammed, Ahmed, or both.*

Profiling of a sort has been an official practice of the nation's airlines for years. In 1994, Northwest began to develop a computer-assisted passenger pre-screening system (CAPPS) to single out high-threat passengers. After the TWA Flight 800 disaster in July 1996, the Clinton administration convened an Al Gore–led commission to study aviation security. This commission recommended that the Northwest system be adopted by the airline industry generally. But, under pressure from Arab-American and civil-liberties groups, it insisted that profiling not rely "on material of a constitutionally suspect nature—e.g., race, religion, or national origin of U.S. citizens." The profiles instead would use factors such as whether someone had bought a one-way ticket or paid cash for it.

Even this prompted howls of outrage. After the commission issued its final recommendations in 1997, a dozen Arab-American and civil-liberties groups sent a letter to Gore warning that "the risks to privacy are enormous" and reminding him that "passengers check their luggage, not their constitutional rights." The ACLU [American Civil Liberties Union] even complained that CAPPS might be biased against poor people, since they may not have credit cards. The Gore commission had gone out of its way to address such concerns: It had convened a group of civil-liberties experts to worry officially about the dangers of profiling in an appendix to its report. "Efforts should be made," the group advised, "to avoid using characteristics that impose a disproportionate burden of inconvenience, embarrassment, or invasion of privacy on members of minority racial, religious, or ethnic groups."

> *Not all terrorists are idiots, so they might attempt to avoid the behavior that triggers the profiling system.*

Efforts to avoid embarrassment were indeed vigorous. And this is why there was eventually some Arab-American support for CAPPS. The Justice Department examined CAPPS in 1997 for evidence of racism, and found none, although it recommended that the FAA [Federal Aviation Administration] require airlines to take steps to keep profiling from becoming discriminatory or insensitive. The FAA obliged, focusing on preventing personal searches that might make flagged passengers feel uncomfortable. "Manual screening has been criticized by persons who perceived it as discriminating against citizens on the basis of race, color, national or ethnic origin and gender," warned the FAA.

Sensitive Profiling

No one flagged by CAPPS, therefore, would be searched on their persons, so they wouldn't even know they had been profiled. Instead, their checked luggage might be screened for bombs, and attempts might be made to ensure they actually boarded the plane on which they checked their bags (the pre–September 11 assumption was that no terrorist would get on the same plane as a bomb). The feds had hit on a perfect policy: sensitive, hands-free profiling! This politically correct system had its intended politically correct result: According to the Council on American-Islamic Relations, profiling complaints dropped from 27 when CAPPS first came online in 1997, to two in 1999, and finally none in 2000.

> *It is inarguable that sensitivity about profiling in the U.S. made the September 11 hijackers' job easier.*

CAPPS, then, had served its political function. Its security function was another matter. Not all terrorists are idiots, so they might attempt to avoid the behavior that triggers the profiling system. For example, they can buy round-trip tickets and use credit—thus easily slipping by two of the CAPPS criteria. According to the *Wall Street Journal*, CAPPS managed to flag two of the September 11 hijackers, Nawaf Alhazmi and Khalid Al-Midhar, who commandeered Flight 77, the Pentagon plane. They had reserved their tickets by credit card, but paid in cash. While their checked bags were supposedly more carefully checked, neither of them was searched or questioned at the airport—lest, presumably, they complain to the Council on American-Islamic Relations.

And so, they went on their way. If ethnicity and national origin were among the CAPPS criteria, all of the September 11 hijackers probably would have been flagged. And, as the Manhattan Institute's Heather Mac Donald has pointed out, if personal searches and questioning had been routine, a bizarre pattern might have become clear—why so many Arabs in first class? why so many box cutters?—and the whole plot come undone. Other countries have had exactly this experience. In a famous 1986 case, a pregnant woman booked on an El Al flight from Heathrow to Tel Aviv was pulled aside (pregnant women don't usually travel alone). After questioning, it was discovered that, unbeknownst to her, her Jordanian boyfriend had planted a bomb in her carry-on bag that would have killed all 375 people on her flight. It is inarguable that sensitivity about profiling in the U.S. made the September 11 hijackers' job easier.

Their plot would have simply been a non-starter in Israel. There, passengers are divided into three categories: Israelis and foreign Jews, non-Jewish foreigners, and anyone with an Arab name. Those in the third category get lots of special attention, including being taken to a special room for baggage and body checks. Arab passengers can be interrogated up to three different times. The philosophy is to concentrate resources on the more likely threats, and not waste them on low-risk passengers. As one former Israeli security official told the Associated Press, if everyone got the most vigorous treatment, the planes would never get off the ground.

> *The Israeli system requires a tough-mindedness that is in short supply in the U.S.*

But the Israeli system requires a tough-mindedness that is in short supply in the U.S. On the issue of profiling, transportation secretary Norman Mineta's ignorance appears to be nearly invincible. Mineta's Japanese-American family was interned during World War II. He implies at every opportunity that by standing in the way of ethnic profiling, he is preventing a similar enormity today. "A very basic foundation to all of our work," he says, "is to make sure that racial profiling is not part of it." Asked on *60 Minutes* if a 70-year-old white woman from Vero Beach should receive the same level of scrutiny as a Muslim from Jersey City, Mineta said, "Basically, I would hope so."

Lazy Thinking

Mineta pulls no rhetorical punches: "Surrendering to actions of hate and discrimination makes us no different than the despicable terrorists who rained such hatred on our people." Since Mineta thinks "discrimination" includes ethnic profiling, this must be one of the laziest statements of post–September 11 moral equivalence this side of [essayist and novelist] Susan Sontag. The airlines are only too happy to play along. A September 21 [2001] memo to Delta employees from CEO Fred Reid has the subject line "Tolerance," and disavows ethnic profiling in the strongest possible terms: "We cannot afford to follow this tragic behavior. It is exactly what our enemies are striving for: the end of our open, diverse, and tolerant way of life."

If you believe the feds, the airlines have a legal obligation to ape the federal line. In memos sent to the airlines after September 11, the Transportation Department has constantly claimed that the law forbids profiling on the basis of ethnicity or national origin: "Various federal statutes prohibit air carriers from subjecting a person in air transportation to discrimination on the basis of race, color, national origin, religion, sex, or ancestry." I called a spokesman at Transportation to confirm that the department meant to suggest that ethnic profiling constituted illegal discrimination. He was adamant that this was so.

But this is, at best, a misreading of the law. Discrimination in public conveyances has been outlawed for a long time, but that was meant to forbid things like forcing blacks to ride on the back of the bus. The circumstances of airline security are, of course, entirely different. Profiling at airports would not be classic New Jersey Turnpike "racial profiling," where police mark out a whole class of people as more likely than average to be transporting drugs, and then stop large numbers of them. Airport profiling would respond to a specific threat to commit a specific crime (more suicide hijackings) made by a specific group (the Islamic terrorists of al-Qaeda). It would be less analogous to New Jersey, then, than to a recent case in Oneonta, N.Y. The courts endorsed the right of police there to stop and examine almost every black man in that small town after an elderly woman said she had been attacked by a black assailant whose hand was cut in their scuffle.

> *Profiling at airports would not be classic New Jersey Turnpike 'racial profiling,' where police mark out a whole class of people as more likely than average to be transporting drugs.*

So, the airlines and the federal government are not legally required but instead are freely choosing to collaborate in a system that no one considers secure, while creating the maximum inconvenience and delays. It's a system that features the false egalitarianism of the anti-profilers. One of the recommendations of the Gore commission's in-house anti-profiling panel was that "the procedures applied to those who fit the profile should also be applied on a random basis to some percentage of passengers who do not fit the profile." This idea has been adopted on a massive scale, which accounts for much of the absurdity of flying today: ditzy celebrities, children, and older women subjected to the same excruciating security as a 25-year-old man just arrived from Riyadh.

Terrorist Grandmother

There are many problems with this. The first is one of justice. It burdens people whom we have absolutely no reason to believe have any chance of being terrorists, just to create an appearance at airports that will make young male Arabs feel better. The second is that the time and resources spent getting the proverbial Vero Beach 70-year-old to take off her white sneakers could be better spent searching and questioning a passenger who has a higher chance of being a terrorist. Finally, there is the matter of economics.

> *The answer is to separate out passengers according to the threat they represent.*

Long lines make people marginally less likely to fly, which pushes airlines that much closer to bankruptcy. The only way to reduce lines in the current system would be to add more security checkpoints. But that's not easy. It means hiring more screeners, when it is difficult to have enough competent ones to fill the current slots; it means spending more money, when airlines are already bleeding; and it bumps up against a physical constraint at many airports, which may not have more room for screening checkpoints. The same problem applies to examining checked luggage—there is so much of it and so few machines that doing all of it well and quickly will be impractical for years.

It obviously makes sense to find ways to whittle down the security load. The answer is to separate out passengers according to the threat they represent, probably into three groups. One would be members of an enhanced frequent-flyer program, with travelers voluntarily undergoing a background check and getting a fool-proof biometric ID card in return for fewer security hassles. (The airport in Amsterdam already has such a program, which includes an eye scan.) Arab-American travelers could opt into such a program, and never again worry about being profiled. Then, there would be the unwashed masses, who would get more routine security treatment. The last category would be passengers profiled as potential risks, who could get a version of the full-bore Israeli scrutiny.

This would make everyone involved very uncomfortable, especially, of course, the targeted passengers. Almost all of them would be clean. The extra burden on young male Arab-Americans and Arab immigrants—the extra pat-down, the searching questions—would be very unfair in a cosmic sense, but an acceptable social cost given the stakes involved in preventing further attacks.

Pilots' Rights

The fact that no one is systemically profiled on the basis of ethnicity and national origin now contributes to the nervousness of pilots, passengers, and security personnel who don't trust the current system and attempt to do amateur profiling on their own. A sophisticated computerized system would reduce the need for individual judgments after a passenger has already passed security checkpoints. But a pilot should still have the right to refuse a passenger, a privilege that goes back to old maritime law. It was this prerogative that was in play in the American Airlines/Secret Service agent case, as the pilot balked at carrying an agitated armed man whose paperwork wasn't properly filled out.

American, to its credit, has stood by the pilot, all the while insisting that the airline would never ethnically profile. But if the pilot hadn't noticed that the angry guy trying to board his plane with a gun looked like all of the September 11 terrorists, he would have been a fool. The Left talks often of "diversity," but is unwilling to acknowledge that the world's variousness might mean that certain ethnic groups are more likely to be terrorists than others. Willfully ignoring this fact contributed to September 11. Continuing to do so would heap criminal folly on top of willful recklessness. In a famous 1949 case, Justice Robert Jackson said that the Constitution is not "a suicide pact." Indeed, it isn't, but maybe our racial politics is.

4

Racial Profiling Does Not Increase Border Security

Amnesty International

*Amnesty International is a Nobel Prize–winning activist or-
ganization founded in 1961 to research, end, and prevent
human rights abuses worldwide. The organization, with an
estimated 1.8 million members in 150 countries, is not af-
filiated with any government or religion and neither supports
nor opposes the views of the victims whose rights it seeks to
protect. After a yearlong study, in September 2004 Amnesty
International released its first-ever report on the prevalence
and effects of racial profiling in the United States, from
which the following article is excerpted.*

Since the September 11, 2001, terrorist attacks, U.S. law
enforcement agencies have targeted people of Muslim,
South Asian, and Middle Eastern descent for searches,
detention, and deportation in an effort to tighten the
borders against terrorists and other criminals. Such
racial profiling is ineffective as well as unfair. Not only
does it frighten and antagonize innocent people and
disrupt their communities, it fails to identify threats,
because skin color, religion, and ethnicity are unreliable
predictors of criminal behavior. Until immigration services and law enforcement authorities shift their focus
from racial characteristics to suspect behaviors, America
will be increasingly vulnerable to attack by people who
do not fit criminal or terrorist stereotypes.

R acial profiling is a human rights violation that can affect Americans in virtually every sphere of their daily lives and often has an impact that goes far beyond the initial incident. . . . This seemingly ubiquitous human rights violation leaves its victims feeling humiliated, depressed, helpless, and angry. Furthermore, racial profiling reinforces residential segregation, creates fear and mistrust, and engenders reluctance in reporting crimes and cooperating with police officers. In these times of domestic insecurity, our nation simply cannot afford to tolerate practices and policies that build walls between individuals or communities and those who are charged with the duty of protecting all of us.

> *From a domestic security perspective, the bottom line is that nobody knows what the next terrorist, serial killer, or smuggler will look like.*

From a domestic security perspective, the bottom line is that nobody knows what the next terrorist, serial killer, or smuggler will look like. In Washington DC, as this study was being designed in the offices of the U.S. Domestic Human Rights Program of AIUSA [Amnesty International USA], the staff and thousands of other innocent area residents were forced to live in fear for several days as two snipers randomly killed local residents. The police, apparently operating on the standard profile of a serial killer, told the public to be on the look out for an antisocial white male, probably traveling alone. Later they suggested this individual was possibly driving a white van. They ended up arresting, and ultimately convicting, two African-American males in a blue car. Later in 2003, while the staff was reviewing multiple complaints from Arab and South Asian Americans about being profiled at airports, news stories appeared about a white college student from Maryland who was able to sneak box cutters, knives, and a substance resembling plastic explosives onto six airplanes without being detected by airport security officials. Then, as the report was being drafted and more than a year after native-born British citizen Richard Reid had been arrested for trying to ignite a shoe bomb on a trans-Atlantic airline, came reports that Federal officials were searching for "European-looking" Al Qaeda operatives. Unfortunately, a virtually simultaneous announcement that the FBI was closely monitoring thousands of Muslims in the U.S., as well as related complaints that continue to be received by several civil rights organizations, suggest that federal authorities continue to target people of Middle Eastern and South Asian descent for scrutiny in airports and other contexts. While this ineffective and unfair targeting may give some the illusion of safety, it actually makes us all less safe.

The people of the United States of America continue to pay a price for the failure of their leadership and law enforcement agencies to fully learn the lesson that judgments made essentially on the basis of skin color, hair texture, gender, nation of origin, faith are an unreliable basis for determining which individuals to monitor, search, or question. Similarly, historical examples—from the assassination of President [William] McKinley to the ongoing "War on Terror"—suggest that racial profiling diverts law enforcement's attention away from criminal behavior in ways that ultimately put the welfare of the nation, its citizens, and its leadership at risk. . . .

Traveling Through Airports

Since September 11, 2001 there has been a widely reported increase in racial profiling at airports, particularly as it applies to people who appear to be Muslim or of South Asian or Middle-Eastern descent. In Tulsa, Dr. Sandra Rana, a member of the Tulsa Police Community Race Relations Committee, told us about her family's experience at the airport.

> *While this ineffective and unfair targeting may give some the illusion of safety, it actually makes us all less safe.*

Dr. Rana described how airport officials targeted her family, pulling her eight-year-old son from the line and taking apart the Boy Scout pinewood derby car he had built. Her son, Omar, is now routinely targeted at airports. Dr. Rana explained,

> Imagine how I felt when my eight-year-old son was pulled from the line because of his name and I could not go with him. Imagine how he felt when

they started to take apart his Boy Scout pinewood derby car in the Boy Scout box. . . . It is now routine for my son, for Omar Rana, to get extra security checks at the airport. He knows it's going to happen, and he expects it. . . . But how do I tell my . . . son that it's okay? He is now ten. He is learning about civil liberties and civil rights. What meaning do they have for him. . . ?

Upon advice from law enforcement officials, Dr. Rana has stopped wearing her *hijab* to the airport (*hijab* is the traditional Muslim head covering for women),

It's not just the scarf. I tell my kids, don't speak Urdu. It's the Pakistani language. Don't speak it when you're on the plane. Don't take the Quran. We've been advised by officials, do not carry any book that's in Arabic. . . . Don't do anything that will cause attention to yourself.

Indeed, even long-time airport employees have been targeted while traveling on family vacations. Consider the testimony of Mahmoud El Rosoul, a Muslim American citizen, from the hearings in Dallas.

> *Skin color, hair texture, gender, nation of origin, faith are an unreliable basis for determining which individuals to monitor, search, or question.*

Mr. El Rosoul has been working as an engineer for a major airline company for 22 years. In March 2003, on their way back from a vacation in Hawaii, Mr. El Rosoul and his family were stopped at the checkpoint because their tickets were marked by American Airlines. They were pulled out of line and every one of them, including his nine-year-old, eight-year-old and four-year-old children, were thoroughly searched. The lengthy search caused them to miss their flight, and they were forced to spend the night in the airport at Los Angeles. Mr. El Rosoul is disheartened especially because he has spent 22 years building airplane engines for the airline that treated him so poorly. He says, "They think [the September 11, 2001, terrorist attacks are] our fault. We have to take responsibility for [them]. . . . They think America is going to be a better country without us."

> **The National Security Entry-Exit Registration System (NSEERS) . . . spurred thousands of long-term visitors to the United States to seek asylum in Canada and other nations.**

Some people report being profiled because of multiple personal characteristics. At the hearings in New York City we heard from Mr. Herb Boyd, a reporter with *Amsterdam News*, whose testimony illustrates how the intersectionality of race and religious or ethnic appearance can often make individuals "doubly suspicious":

Mr. Boyd often wears Islamic garments. He describes his experience at airports after the attacks of September 11, 2001,

> During a flight to Detroit in December 2001, I noticed that my ticket had a red dot on it. I didn't pay any attention to that until I discovered I was standing with several others, all of them identifiably Arabs or [of] Arab descent. We were all virtually stripped before entering the plane. Two of [them] . . . told me they had endured such searches every flight they took. What I was to learn in successive flights is that a black man carrying a Kufi or Arabic garments was doubly suspicious. So any perverse satisfaction I may have momentarily derived from not being the main target of racial profiling in [post–September 11, 2001] America gradually vanished. . . .

Selectively Chosen Deportees and Their Families

Following the attacks of September 11, 2001, the U.S. Government immediately enacted policies and took actions directed at Arabs, Muslims, and people of Middle-Eastern and South-Asian descent. These practices—often carried out through selective enforcement of immigration laws—have led to the deportation of thousands of men and boys from these communities, the disruption of family and community life, and the economic devastation of thousands of otherwise law-abiding citizens and immigrants.

In the immediate aftermath of the attacks, immigration and law enforcement officials targeted immigrants from predominantly Arab and Muslim countries for selective enforcement of immigration laws as part of a nationwide attempt to find possible terrorism suspects. More than 1,200 non-U.S. nationals were detained as a result. None have been publicly charged with terrorism. In June 2003, a report released by the Department of Justice's Office of the Inspector General . . . confirmed Amnesty International's prior reports that hundreds of men detained in the roundup were deprived of many of their rights and experienced physical and mental abuse at the hands of prison guards in the detention center.

> **NSEERS policy targeted many law-abiding and productive members of U.S. society.**

In 2002, the introduction of the National Security Entry-Exit Registration System (NSEERS or "Special Registration") for visiting males ages 16 and over from 24 predominantly Muslim countries (and North Korea) literally spurred thousands of long-term visitors to the United States to seek asylum in Canada and other nations. The program, which called for visitors already in the U.S. to be registered and interrogated, appeared to use nationality as a proxy for their religion and ethnicity. While we are no longer faced with the visible spectacle of thousands of terrified men and boys lining up at immigration offices around the country trying to meet their group's call-in date, the program continues to have a powerful impact on the communities and families of the more than 13,000 men and boys who have been already deported or are still in deportation proceedings due to having been discriminatorily chosen for enforcement of immigration laws. Many of these individuals with minor immigration violations had applications pending to regularize their status, but were stuck in long backlogs with the U.S. immigration service. Moreover, while initially Department of Justice officials said that this program would be extended to visitors from every country, it was canceled once visitors from these 25 countries had been called in.

Shortly after NSEERS was enacted, affected communities around the U.S. lost large portions of their male population, resulting in the rapid impoverishment and destabilization of many families. To avoid "Special Registration" and the possibility of its ensuing negative consequences, many individuals from targeted immigrant communities fled with their families to the Canadian border. According to Suhail Muzaffar, president of the Federation of Associations of Pakistani Americans, new immigration policies created a panic within Pakistani-American communities, causing some to close their businesses and flee to Canada to seek refuge from what they believed to be "religious persecution." Mr. Muzaffar also said that many Pakistanis were depressed, confused and did not show up to register.

In addition to disrupting immigrants' lives, NSEERS policy targeted many law-abiding and productive members of U.S. society and, in some cases, caused them to leave the country. Nabil K. has a Master's in Business Administration from an Ivy League university and worked on New York's Wall Street for over five years. After the NSEERS policy was announced, Nabil moved back to Karachi, Pakistan "for the sake of dignity."

NSEERS and other post-9/11 immigration policies have indeed had a negative impact on the U.S. economy. Secretary of State Colin Powell and head of the Department of Homeland Security Tom Ridge both have recently admitted that post–September 11, 2001, immigration policies have hurt the economy by leading to a 30 percent decline in overseas visits to the U.S. Additionally, the number of foreign students in universities is also down, as are visits by businessmen, scientists, and other scholars. . . .

Domestic Security Impact of Over-Generalized Suspicion

Racial profiling is a liability in the effort to make our nation safer. Race-based policing practices have frequently distracted law enforcement officials and made them blind to dangerous behaviors and real threats. Moreover, this is a lesson that law enforcement should have internalized a long time ago. To help illustrate the grave cost of racial profiling as an intended guard against acts of international and domestic terror, we offer two historical examples. The first is from the opening of the twentieth century; the second is from the opening of the twenty-first: . . .

[In] September 1901, President McKinley was murdered by Leon Czolgosz, an American-born native of Michigan, who concealed a pistol in a bandage that was wrapped around his arm and hand so it looked like it covered a wound or broken bone. Secret Service agent George Foster was assigned to search individuals coming to the area where President McKinley would be greeting members of the public. He later admitted to having chosen not to search Czolgosz because he was focused on a "dark complexioned man with a black moustache" who was behind Czolgosz in the line of people coming through Foster's checkpoint. Agent Forester tried to explain his actions by telling investigators that the "colored man" made him feel suspicious. When asked "Why?" he replied, "I didn't like his general appearance." Ironically, it was later revealed that the man whose complexion had so captivated the agent's attention was the same person who saved President McKinley from a third bullet and apprehended the assassin—Jim Parker, an African-American former constable who attended the event as a spectator. Mr. Parker's act of heroism was widely credited with extending the President's life for several days. As a result of reliance on racial stereotypes, the agent on duty overlooked Czolgosz, who despite his foreign-sounding last name—not to mention, his avowed allegiance to the anarchist cause—looked like "a mechanic out for the day to the Exposition.". . .

> *Post–September 11, 2001, immigration policies have hurt the economy by leading to a 30 percent decline in overseas visits to the U.S.*

During the 2002 sniper attacks in the DC area, police officers were looking for a disaffected white man acting alone or with a single accomplice (the standard profile of a serial killer). After several subsequent reports, they focused their search on white males driving white vans. Police officers conducting surveillance and searches throughout the metropolitan area—including those at each of the multiple roadblocks that were quickly put up after most of the shootings—used this general description of the suspect and the suspect's vehicle. At one point, due to mistaken leads about Middle-Eastern terrorists, the FBI began planning to question Al-Qaeda prisoners held at

Guantánamo Bay, Cuba for possible information on the snipers. Meanwhile, police came in contact with the African-American man and boy—who were ultimately accused, tried, and convicted for the crimes—at least ten times and did not apprehend them because, according to DC homicide detective Tony Patterson, "everybody just got tunnel vision." The suspects' blue Chevrolet Caprice was spotted near one of the shooting scenes, and was stopped several times by police, yet the snipers were able to escape every time with the alleged murder weapons in their possession. Officials were so focused on race that they failed to notice that one of the snipers, John Allen Muhammad, possessed many of the other characteristics often associated with serial killers (i.e., military background, angry, divorced, lost custody of children, etc.). As former FBI Agent Candace DeLong put it, "A black sniper? That was the last thing I was thinking."

> *Race-based policing practices have frequently distracted law enforcement officials and made them blind to dangerous behaviors and real threats.*

In each case, the United States paid a clear price for law enforcement officers thinking that they knew what an otherwise unidentified threat looked like. In the first instance, the U.S. president was assassinated, in part, because his Secret Service agents were apparently relying on stereotypes of what an "international anarchist" looked like. In the second, millions of residents of the Washington, DC metropolitan area were terrorized for several days as the serial killers repeatedly evaded police, in part because officers were relying upon scientifically-supported profiles that speculated the assailants were white. As DC Police Chief Charles Ramsey pointed out, "We were looking for a white van with white people, and we ended up with a blue car with black people." In each instance, officers' ability to focus on and detect dangerous behaviors (a pistol in the bandaged hand of a white male passing through a Secret Service checkpoint; a rifle in the trunk of the car of two African-American males who repeatedly came in contact with police engaged in the search for a serial sniper) was apparently compromised by the distraction of the assailants' race. . . .

In October 2003, Nathaniel Heatwole, a white college student from North Carolina, was charged with a felony for smuggling knives, box cutters, bleach, and items with the same consistency as plastic explosives onto six Southwest Airlines flights. These items were not discovered for over a month, despite the fact that Mr. Heatwole sent numerous e-mail messages to the Transportation and Security Administration informing them of his actions. After they were discovered on two planes, Heatwole told authorities he had actually successfully smuggled such items onto those two and four more. Heatwole claimed that this was an act of civil disobedience intended to improve security measures for airline travelers. . . .

Failing to Learn from Past Mistakes

Several of the United States' domestic "War on Terror" strategies (such as the post-9/11 attack roundups of Muslim and Arab men in New York City and the National Security Entry/Exit Registration Program) appear to have been conceived without appreciation for past mistakes. Moreover, incidents described earlier in this report suggest a general failure of many American law enforcement agencies and officers to learn sufficiently from our country's historical mistakes. They also suggest a failure to internalize the complexity of our nation's current domestic security situation. While a wide range of "post–September 11, 2001" policies and practices seem to be informed by the fact that all of the 19 hijackers on the day of the attacks were Middle-Eastern males, U.S. law enforcement seems often to have acted in ways that ignore the facts that: (a) the overwhelming majority of people who belong to Arab-American, Muslim-American, and South-Asian-American communities are innocent and law abiding, and (b) many of the Al-Qaeda sympathizers detained since have come from a wide range of other ethnic groups and nationalities (such as Chicano-American Jose Padilla, white American Taliban combatant John Walker Lindh, and the British "shoe-bomber" Richard Reid).

What is more, the decision to focus, even partially, on racial characteristics instead of on behaviors runs counter to a significant lesson learned from one of the most relevant changes in U.S. airport security policy in the last ten years. In the 1990s, spurred by discrimination lawsuits, the U.S. Customs Service eliminated the use of race in deciding which individuals to stop and search and instead began relying on a list of suspect behaviors. According to a study of U.S. Customs by Lamberth Consulting, the policy shift to color-blind profiling techniques increased the rate of productive searches—searches that led to discovery of illegal contraband or activity—by more than 300 percent.

If history is any judge, the impact of this failure to forgo the distraction of race-based strategies means that all Americans will continue to be at risk of attacks by individuals whose physical appearance or ethnicity defies popular stereotypes about terrorist conspirators. Meanwhile, law enforcement resources will continue to be squandered on over-scrutinizing millions of American citizens and visitors, ultimately because of how they look, where they or their ancestors are from, or what they wear.

5

The Military Should Defend the U.S. Border

Carlton Meyer

Carlton Meyer is a former U.S. Marine Corps officer and the editor of the military affairs Web site www.g2mil.com.

Many Americans believe that using soldiers to defend the border is illegal or unconstitutional. This is a myth. The U.S. Army's main role in peacetime before World War II was patrolling the Mexican border. Only 2 percent of the standing army would be needed to deploy along federal lands on the border, and several existing bases could be used to support their mission. With proper training and focus on repelling potential invaders, the army would be an effective force that cuts down on illegal aliens once the word got out that the U.S. border is no longer unprotected.

The corporate media in the USA is extremely powerful and dumbs down all Americans. They want cheap labor pouring across US borders to drive down worker wages, so they invent simple phrases to confuse Americans. "We are a nation of immigrants" is a meaningless phrase used to end rational discussion about what is best for the American people. England and Mexico are also nations of immigrants. In fact, most scientists agree that man originated from a spot in Africa, so every nation on Earth is a nation of immigrants and everyone's ancestors were immigrants. Even the misnamed "native Americans" came from Asia, albeit a few thousand years before those from Europe. To keep the gates for cheap labor open, corporate television along with corporate sponsored politicians have used irrational slogans to convince many Americans that putting US troops on the border is unconstitutional, illegal, impractical, dangerous, and futile. Let us review these myths:

> **The Constitution clearly requires the federal government to protect states from invasion.**

Myth #1 The US Constitution prohibits posting US troops on the border.

The US Constitution says no such thing. In fact, Article VI states:

Section 4. The United States shall guarantee to every state in this union a republican form of government, and shall protect each of them against invasion; and on application of the legislature, or of the executive (when the legislature cannot be convened) against domestic violence.

So the Constitution clearly requires the federal government to protect states from invasion. Over a half million aliens illegally pouring across the border into states each year is clearly an invasion.

Myth #2 The Posse Comitatus Act prohibits US troops from guarding US borders.

This 1878 act was enacted to prevent Union troops from continuing to enforce federal law in the defeated South after the American Civil War. Here is the text as modified by Congress in recent years:

Sec. 1385.—Use of Army and Air Force as posse comitatus

Whoever, except in cases and under circumstances expressly authorized by the Constitution or Act of Congress, willfully uses any part of the Army or the Air Force as a posse comitatus or otherwise to execute the laws shall be fined under this title or imprisoned not more than two years, or both.

Foreign Invasion

Guarding US borders from foreign invasion is not "domestic law enforcement". The US Army exists to defend the US from foreign invasion which is expressly authorized by the Constitution. Guarding the Mexican border was the Army's primary peacetime mission until 1940, and no one ever declared this was in violation of this 1878 act. The US Border Patrol wasn't even formed until 1924, so claiming the intent of this law was to prevent Army troops from protecting the border is absurd. . . .

Some may argue that Chapter 18, Section 375 of Title 10 US Code prevents military personnel from direct participation in law enforcement. However, defending US borders from foreign invaders is not law enforcement, it's the basic purpose of the US military. While defending these United States from invasion, civilian law enforcement may be called upon to assist the US military. Does anyone believe the Border Patrol must operate fighter aircraft because the US Air Force can't intercept aircraft crossing into the US because that's "domestic law enforcement"?

When you read about proposals in Congress to put US troops on the border, those are not proposals to allow US troops on the border, but proposals to force the President to put troops back on the border. However, recent Presidents have listened to their corporate advisors and their slogans and ignored the threat of unsecured US borders.

> *Guarding the US border is a full-time mission which the federal government is required to perform by Article IV of the US Constitution.*

Myth #3 The National Guard should guard the border, not active duty troops.

The National Guard is an organized militia to deal with state and national emergencies. Guarding the US border is a full-time mission which the federal government is required to perform by Article IV of the US Constitution. The few states along the border shouldn't be expected to defend the entire country from invasion. This myth is also spread by imperial minded Generals who prefer to rule an empire overseas than to defend their own citizens. Whenever citizens demand the Army protect their nation, Generals dodge this issue by stating it may be a mission for the National Guard, to be funded by states so as not to waste resources of the US Army. This is absurd; the primary mission of the US Army is to protect US citizens, and the US Constitution requires the federal government to protect states from invasion. If there is a major war and the

Army would like to deploy its border troops overseas, then National Guard troops from any state can be mobilized to guard the border until the war ends.

Myth #4 The US Army hasn't the resources for border troops.

The active duty army has 480,000 full-time troops supported by over 300,000 civilians. The Border Patrol has 9700 agents. Certainly, the Army can form a infantry division of 10,000 troops to actually defend the USA, or Congress can authorize more troops. This *G2mil* article: "Cut Surplus Army Units" identifies more than 10,000 unneeded positions in the US Army that can be cut to form an infantry division. There are several US military bases along the border which can host an infantry battalion for border security: NAS [Naval Air Station] Whidbey Island, WA; Minot AFB [Air Force Base], SD; Selfridge ARNG [Army National Guard] base, MI; Fort Drum, NY; Laughlin AFB, TX; Fort Bliss, TX; Fort Huachuca, AZ; Yuma Proving Grounds, AZ; and NAS El Centro, CA; plus several military facilities in the San Diego area. Some Army officers may express concern that border duty will hurt readiness for real Army missions overseas. They just don't understand that defending the USA is their real mission!

Myth #5 Soldiers aren't trained for such missions

Soldiers are ideally trained to guard remote areas of the border. All they need are a few days of orientation training and to learn some Spanish or French phrases they can shout into a bullhorn: "Stop, you cannot enter the United States here, go back!" They will not process arrestees, fill out paperwork, search houses, run checkpoints, appear in court, or conduct investigations. They will just confront people who they directly view invading the USA. They will insist that aliens turn back or face arrest by the Border Patrol.

> *Few Americans know that most of the US border is not guarded at all and vehicles routinely drive across.*

This will prevent odd incidents like in 1997 when a Marine on drug war duty near the border shot a local goat herder who had fired in his direction. Marines were there because the President had authorized their use after Army Generals refused. The

Marine shooter was there on temporary duty and did not view the victim entering the USA illegally. The establishment of orientation training and strict rules of engagement can ensure US troops have no contact with US citizens.

> *Border patrol agents are so busy rounding up aliens they haven't the time, equipment, nor motivation to conduct dangerous squad-size combat patrols into the wilderness.*

Myth #6 Illegal immigration cannot be stopped

Of course it can. There is no illegal immigration from North to South Korea because that border is heavily guarded. Perhaps some of the 38,000 US troops there can transfer to the US border. Guarding the border will not stop the hundreds of thousands visitors who overstay their visas in the USA, but at least they were checked and inspected prior to arrival. The Border Patrol estimates that 700,000 unknown persons slipped past them last year, cutting that to 7000 a year is not unrealistic. Some claim that illegals will "just find another way to cross". However, most illegals cannot obtain a visa or shopping pass because they haven't an address and job.

Unguarded Frontiers

While the corporate media keeps Americans confused with slogans, it never reports on the problems of illegal immigration, except for Bill O'Reilly at Fox. As a result, few Americans know that most of the US Border is not guarded at all and vehicles routinely drive across. In May 2002, the US Immigration and Naturalization Service was required to pay back wages and cancel suspension and demotion orders for two Border Patrol agents who told a newspaper about security problems along the US-Canadian border. The agents, assigned to the INS field office in Detroit, were recommended for discipline after they told the *Detroit Free Press* that Michigan's border lacked the resources to adequately protect the country from terrorists. Agents Mark Hall and Robert Lindemann said the 804 miles of shoreline border were guarded by 28 field agents, one working boat, several damaged electronic sensors and one broken remote camera. Keep in mind that these 28 field agents must cover that 804 miles of border 24 hours a day, seven days a week, plus days off for vacation or illness. So there are only about six on duty at any given time, or three teams of two. Then when a team catches someone, they must transport and book him, so they're gone for hours.

Another major problem is that guarding remote areas of the border is a tough mission, which is not compatible with the unionized Border Patrol. They prefer to work 8-hour shifts and their union contract requires the government to provide them with proper meals and lodging when away from home. Since it can take hours to reach remote areas from the nearest Border Patrol station, it's not practical to guard vast areas of the border. As a result, agents set up roadblocks or cruise around roadways rounding up who they can. This is much more interesting than standing a post along the border all day. However, the effort becomes pointless as it requires hours for the Border Patrol to process each arrested alien, who is then released on the other side of the border and walks back across for another try. In some urban sectors, the Border Patrol has focused on deterrence by placing most agents right on the border to stand guard. However, this becomes boring and dirty, which accounts for the high turnover rate among Border Patrol agents.

> *" Unlike canned peacetime exercises, the border is real and unpredictable. "*

Another reason much of the border is not patrolled is that it's too dangerous. Last year [2003], six Mexican Army Hummers were two miles inside US territory when Mexican soldiers fired over 150 rounds from vehicle-mounted machine guns, and a dozen MK-19 40mm grenade rounds, at two US Border Patrol agents investigating narcotics trafficking in the Buenos Aires National Wildlife refuge north of Sasebe, Arizona. It is well known that some of the Mexican Army is involved in drug smuggling and Mexican troops are frequently encountered on the US side of the border in remote areas; see the great movie "Traffic" with Michael Douglas. [In 2002], a US Park Ranger was killed when drug smugglers sprayed him with bullets from an AK-47, which struck him just below his bullet proof vest. With rogue Mexican army troops chasing off Border Patrol agents, Park Rangers wearing bullet proof vests, and thousands of recently deported criminal aliens walking back across, isn't it time for the US Army to return to the border?

Border Patrol agents are so busy rounding up aliens they haven't the time, equipment, nor motivation to conduct dangerous squad-size combat patrols into the wilderness. Most Border Patrol agents are hard working and dedicated, but the US Army is better organized for conducting combat patrols and continual surveillance along remote areas of the border. Once the Army sends squads to watch remote areas of the border, Army Generals will be shocked at the number of firefights that break out. Armed smugglers have used routes through remote areas for decades and will be surprised to encounter stealthy soldiers who are undeterred by their AK-47s. The Army will only guard rural border areas and only detain people they observe crossing illegally until Border Patrol agents arrive. This will allow the Border Patrol to focus on running checkpoints, guarding urban areas, and processing arrestees. This is no small task considering the Border Patrol has made over 500,000 arrests since the 9-11 terror attacks.

Remote Duty

Squads of soldiers can deploy to the field for days at a time. A pattern of 72 hours in the field; 72 hours off; 72 hours in garrison for admin and training would work great. This allows an infantry battalion with four line companies to rotate three of them so one is always guarding the border. Each company will go "off line" three months a year for leave, and some traditional infantry training to break up the routine. Since soldiers are transferred every three or four years, they will not face the boring prospect of watching the border for 30 years like Border Patrol agents.

Each border infantry battalion should be supported by a helicopter detachment for emergency medivacs and to move a reaction squad to where shooting has broken out. Some areas may be so remote that helicopters will be needed to rotate squads every three days. However, in most cases troops will be deployed to screen the flanks of border crossings to thwart the common game of just walking around a checkpoint and meeting up with their driver down the road. Squads are likely to rotate to different posts each month to keep border duty interesting.

This will provide great training for soldiers. Unlike canned peacetime exercises, the border is real and unpredictable. Border troops will become experts in map reading, surveillance, field living, and stealthy movement. Their goal will not be to arrest aliens, but confront aliens near the border and turn them back. Anyone who is suspicious or uncooperative can be detained for the Border Patrol. Soldiers will enjoy the mission of actually protecting the USA, and probably engage in a few shoot outs during their border tour of duty. The first year of border duty will be especially chaotic as soldiers regain control of the wild frontier. Eventually, word will spread that crossing the US border is very difficult and problems will subside.

> *The United States has the only army on Earth which thinks defending its nation from invasion is not their role.*

Four rules of engagement can ensure that soldiers do not clash with innocent US citizens:

1) Soldiers will not enter private property without permission of the landowner.

The Border Patrol is legally allowed to enter private property along the border without permission. Most all landowners are happy that someone is protecting their property. However, a few will protest if US troops camp out on their land, and radical groups will sue claiming 3rd Amendment rights are violated. So its best to leave those few alone and let the Border Patrol deal with each issue. There have been cases where smugglers purchased US property on the border to help their operations, so they'd object to US troops too. Since a quarter of the land along the Mexican border is already Federal property, US troops can stay busy just guarding federal lands. Patrolling American parks along the border has become so dangerous that park rangers are twice more likely to suffer injuries from an assault than DEA agents overseas.

2) Soldiers will only conduct surveillance on Mexico, Canada, or international waters to detect persons entering the USA illegally. They will not conduct intelligence missions at targets within the USA, even at the request of law enforcement agencies.

Avoiding Citizens

Many law enforcement agencies work along the border and may ask soldiers to keep an eye on a certain house or building or person they are investigating on the US side of the border. This may seem harmless, but it's not a role for soldiers. If soldiers see a crime in progress, they should report that immediately, but they must not become involved in law enforcement investigations or domestic surveillance.

3) Soldiers will only confront or detain persons who they directly observe entering the USA illegally. They will not confront or detain persons who they suspect have crossed the border illegally.

This will eliminate accidental confrontations between local citizens, unless a US citizen knowing[ly] breaks the law by attempting to enter the US illegally, which is probably because he is involved in other illegal activities. Sometimes soldiers will spot a suspicious group of people on the US side who they didn't observe crossing the border. They may be 99% certain this group slipped across the border, but they cannot be certain, so all they can do is to radio the information to the Border Patrol. This restriction will ensure soldiers have no contact with local citizens while on duty, except with property owners along the border who have given permission to guard their land.

4) Soldiers will not directly assist other government agencies along the border on a routine basis.

Some Army officers and government officials may decide that Army manpower can help guard the border by assisting other agencies. For example, helping search cars and trucks, guarding prisoners, or assisting in raids. However, this is not a role for the Army or soldiers. There will be occasional emergencies or natural disasters where soldiers help out like they do near all Army bases. However, soldiers should not be used as a federal manpower pool.

Genuine Threat

While the Army bureaucracy churns out paperwork about "transformation", the greatest need is for the Army to understand the need to defend the USA. While Americans were shocked when 3000 citizens were killed by the 9-11 terror attacks, more Americans have been killed by illegal aliens over the years. While they may not be more violent than US citizens, if they cannot cross the border they cannot harm Americans. Most people who illegally cross the border are desperate and they will do whatever it takes to survive. That may require fake IDs, identify theft, shoplifting, robbery, or the transport and sale of narcotics.

As the US tracks international terrorists, restricts visas from certain countries, and tightens port security, future terrorists are more likely to just walk across the unguarded border. While some people worry about China's military, they should worry about the thousands of Chinese that slip across the border each year. Placing troops on the border will require orders from the US President, yet it is doubtful that Army Generals have made proposals. In contrast, Generals continue to spread the myths described in this article. The United States has the only army on Earth which thinks defending its nation from invasion is not their role. It is time for the US Army to transform and assign 2% of its manpower to its basic mission of defending the USA on the frontier.

6

Militarization of the Border Is a Bad Idea

Gene Healy

Gene Healy is senior editor at the Cato Institute, a nonprofit, libertarian, public policy research foundation in Washington, D.C. He holds a law degree from the University of Chicago Law School, and is the editor of the book Go Directly to Jail: The Criminalization of Almost Everything.

The use of the U.S. military to patrol America's borders is illegal and unwise for several reasons. First, the 1878 Posse Comitatus Act forbids law enforcement officials from employing the U.S. military to enforce the law, reflecting well-grounded fears of standing armies' ability to oppress the people, and the government's inability to check military power. The act does not bar the military from responding to military-style attacks—soldiers must be trained and equipped to react quickly with lethal use of force for just this purpose. However, these are the wrong skills for dealing with civilians along the borders. Effective border control demands a police force trained in legal procedure, investigative skills, and using force only as a last resort. Using soldiers for border protection would lead to violations of civil liberties, civilian injuries and deaths, and military cover-ups of such incidents in the name of national security interests.

As its overwhelming victories in Afghanistan and Iraq have demonstrated, the U.S. military is the most powerful fighting force in human history. In fact, the military has been so brilliantly effective abroad that it is not altogether surprising that many people think it can be equally effective fighting the war on terrorism here at home. Since the September 11, 2001, terrorist attacks, there has been a rising chorus of calls for deploying military personnel on the home front to fight terrorism. In the immediate aftermath of the attacks, troops were stationed in airports, and fighter jets patrolled the skies over New York and Washington. Later, in early 2002, the Pentagon deployed troops on the borders with Canada and Mexico. Even though that border deployment was temporary, it was a blatant violation of federal law—and a disturbing indication that the Bush administration is willing to disregard the law when it gets in the way. . . .

> *The training, mission, and role of the military and police are so dissimilar that . . . we do not, and should not, want the military to act as a police force.*

High-level officials in Congress and the Bush administration have proposed revising or rescinding the Posse Comitatus Act, the 125-year-old law that restricts the government's ability to use the U.S. military as a police force. Sen. John Warner (R-VA), chairman of the Senate Armed Services Committee, has said that the legal doctrine of *posse comitatus* (force of the county) may have had its day. That view was echoed by Gen. Ralph E. Eberhart, who as head of the new Northern Command oversees all military forces within the United States. Eberhart has declared, "We should always be reviewing things like Posse Comitatus . . . if we think it ties our hands in protecting the American people."

The notion that the military is the appropriate institution for fighting terrorism at home, as well as abroad, is ill-conceived. On the home front, there are many tasks for which the military is ill suited and situations in which its deployment would be hazardous to both civilian life and civil liberties.

Americans have long distrusted the idea of soldiers as domestic police officers—a distrust that is reflected in both the Constitution and federal statutory law. Col. Patrick Finnegan, who heads the Department of Law for the U.S. Military Academy, has observed, "The military is designed and trained to defend our country by fighting and killing the enemy, usually faceless, with no individual rights. . . . The training, mission, and role of the military and police are so dissimilar that it is not surprising that we do not, and should not, want the military to act as a police force." . . .

Posse Comitatus and the September 11 Attacks

The phrase *posse comitatus* refers to the sheriff's common-law power to call upon the male population of a county for assistance in enforcing the laws. Enacted by Congress in 1878, the Posse Comitatus Act forbids law enforcement officials to employ the U.S. military for that purpose. The act consists of a single sentence:

> Whoever, except in cases and under circumstances expressly authorized by the Constitution or Act of Congress, willfully uses any part of the Army as a posse comitatus or otherwise to execute the laws shall be fined under this title or imprisoned not more than two years, or both.

Supporters of the act believed it merely affirmed principles that were already embodied in the Constitution. During the congressional debate in 1877, for example, Rep. Richard Townsend of Illinois said that "it was the real design of those who framed our Constitution that the Federal Army should never be used for any purpose but to repel invasion and to suppress insurrection when it became too formidable for the State to suppress it."

> *The Federal Army should never be used for any purpose but to repel invasion and to suppress insurrection.*

In practice, however, the Posse Comitatus Act has a number of limitations and exceptions that make it far from a blanket prohibition on domestic use of the military. First, the courts have held that the phrase "executing the laws" indicates hands-on policing: searching, arresting, and coercing citizens. Thus, the act does not prohibit the military from providing equipment and training to civilian authorities—even though such civil-military cooperation often works to inculcate a dangerous warrior ethos among police officers. Second, the act applies only to Army regulars and federalized National Guardsmen. If Guard units remain under the command of state governors, the act does not apply. Third, the act does not bar the use of federal troops even for hands-on policing, so long as Congress has passed a statutory "exception"—and there are statutory exceptions in place that permit the military to operate domestically where a terrorist attack with nuclear, biological, or chemical weapons threatens imminent loss of human life. Fourth, the courts have long recognized a "military purpose" exception to the act. When the Army is used domestically to achieve a military purpose, it does not violate the act even if the action incidentally aids civilian law enforcement. Thus, if a latter-day Pancho Villa were to invade the United States, the Army could stop him without violating the Posse Comitatus Act. Finally, even though the act has clearly been violated any number of times since its passage, the Department of Justice has never prosecuted anyone for violating the act.

> *An overly simplistic approach to domestic security . . . sees the military as the answer to almost every conceivable terror threat.*

America's experience in the weeks following the September 11 attacks makes it abundantly clear that the Posse Comitatus Act does not "tie the hands" of the military in responding to terrorism. . . .

[For example,] shortly after September 11, the Air Force was given the authority to shoot down civilian airliners in the event of a hijacking. No one suggested that such activity violated the Posse Comitatus Act, and rightly so. The act's proscription against using the military to "execute the laws" does not bar the use of military forces to ward off a military-style attack. If Al Qaeda [terrorists] somehow procured a squadron of Soviet MIGs and attempted a kamikaze run at the White House, no one would suggest deploying police helicopters to "arrest" them. By shooting the planes down, the Air Force would not be violating federal law—it would be doing its job.

The fact that Al Qaeda has decided to turn civilian airliners into missiles doesn't change the legal analysis. An Air Force pilot ordered to down a hijacked plane would not be trying to enforce the District of Columbia's laws against homicide or federal laws against destruction of federal property—he would be defending the capital against military attack.

> *The military is a blunt instrument: effective for destroying enemy troops en masse but ill suited for the fight on the home front, which requires subtler investigative and preventive skills.*

The Posse Comitatus Act did not prohibit the deployment of some 7,000 National Guardsmen at the nation's airports in the aftermath of the 9/11 attacks. Those troops were operating under the command of the state governors and therefore were not covered by the act. Mindful of the possible danger to civilians, in most cases the governors opted to keep the troops unarmed (as one Pennsylvania Guard leader put it, "We don't want any John Waynes").

Of course, whether the use of the Guardsmen was an intelligent deployment of military personnel is another question entirely. Joseph McNamara, former police chief of Kansas City, Missouri, called the Guardsmen's presence "a pretense of doing something." He argued that the troops provided no real security benefit, and leaving them in place for months after the attacks only made people nervous and discouraged them from flying.

Indeed, use of the Guardsmen was emblematic of an overly simplistic approach to domestic security that sees the military as the answer to almost every conceivable terror threat. Florida authorities, for instance, deployed a tank outside Miami International Airport over the Thanksgiving holiday in 2001, as if the next terror attack would come in the form of an Al Qaeda mechanized column, rather than a shoe bomb or a smuggled boxcutter. But what many public officials fail to understand is that the military is a blunt instrument: effective for destroying enemy troops en masse but ill suited for the fight on the home front, which requires subtler investigative and preventive skills. . . .

Yet [Deputy Secretary of Defense Paul] Wolfowitz and other

administration officials have called for rethinking the Posse Comitatus Act. In July 2002 the White House indicated its openness to a new role for the military in providing domestic security; its *National Strategy for Homeland Security* called for a "thorough review of the laws permitting the military to act within the United States." The views expressed by Gen. Eberhart, the newly appointed commander of all U.S. armed forces within North America, are particularly troubling. In October 2002 Eberhart became head of the new Northern Command, responsible for homeland defense—the first time since America's founding that the command of all military personnel in North America has been centralized under a single officer. So long as the military confines itself to its traditional role, the new homeland command is, in itself, no cause for concern. But Gen. Eberhart has repeatedly contemplated a broader role for the military. In September 2002, for example, Eberhart said, "My view has been that Posse Comitatus will constantly be under review as we mature this command." He did not elaborate on what that "maturation" process will entail.

> *The military 'is trained to vaporize, not Mirandize.'*

Gen. Eberhart's openness to domestic military intervention may be a sign of things to come. Already, some troubling new measures that would expand the domestic role of the military are being explored and tested.

Militarizing the Borders

The Pentagon is under increasing pressure from Congress to militarize America's borders with Canada and Mexico. That pressure led to a six-month deployment of some 1,600 federalized National Guardsmen that ended in August 2002, a deployment carried out in violation of the Posse Comitatus Act. Though most of the soldiers were unarmed, the tasks they undertook involved regulation and compulsion of citizens and thus constituted active police work under the Posse Comitatus Act. The Immigration and Naturalization Service's own press release announcing the use of the Guardsmen stated that soldiers assigned to the border would perform "cargo inspections, traffic management, and pedestrian control." Because the soldiers were operating under federal command and performing policing tasks, the deployment was illegal.

> *Unlike the soldiers deployed for the drug war, the troops on border patrol duty would be given arrest authority and allowed to directly engage civilians.*

Although the troops were removed after six months, the pressure for militarization has not abated. Politicians like Rep. Tom Tancredo (R-CO) and Sen. Trent Lott (R-MS) and conservative pundits like Bill O'Reilly and Michelle Malkin have called for armed soldiers to enforce U.S. immigration law. In her [2004] book, *Invasion*, Malkin writes that "at the northern border with Canada . . . every rubber orange cone and measly 'No Entry' sign should immediately be replaced with an armed National Guardsman." Malkin suggests that something in the neighborhood of 100,000 troops would be appropriate.

The problem with such proposals is that the same training that makes soldiers outstanding warriors makes them extremely dangerous as police officers. Lawrence Korb, former assistant secretary of defense in the Reagan administration, put it succinctly: the military "is trained to vaporize, not Mirandize."[1] No one knows that better than the military establishment, which is why the Pentagon has steadfastly resisted calls to station troops on our borders, most recently in the spring of 2002 when members of Congress pushed for border militarization. Pentagon officials raised the possibility of an "unlawful and potentially lethal use of force incident" if the troops were armed. Ultimately, some 1,600 National Guardsmen, most of them unarmed, were placed on the Mexican and Canadian borders for a six-month mission. A Pentagon official told United Press International: "We do not like to do these things. We do them as a matter of last resort. That is why we entered into this undertaking with a specific end date and a specific requirement."

---

1. When police officers arrest a suspect, they must read the suspect his or her rights, often referred to as the Miranda rights.

Military officials are right to worry. U.S. troops have been placed on the borders in the past, as part of the quixotic fight against drug smuggling. Even though those deployments have been limited to surveillance and support roles, they've led to tragedy in the past. In 1997, for example, a Marine anti-drug patrol shot and killed an 18-year-old high school student named Esequiel Hernandez, who was carrying a .22-caliber rifle while tending goats near his family's farm near the Mexican border. Hernandez allegedly fired two shots in the general direction of the Marines, who were hidden in the brush heavily camouflaged, with blackened faces and bodies covered with burlap and leaves. The Marines did not return fire instantly. Nor did they identify themselves, order Hernandez to put down the rifle, or try to defuse the situation. Instead, they tracked Hernandez silently for 20 minutes. When Hernandez raised his rifle again, a Marine shot him. Hernandez bled to death without receiving first aid. An internal Pentagon investigation noted that the soldiers involved in the shooting were ill prepared for contact with civilians, as their military training instilled "an aggressive spirit while teaching basic combat skills." That assessment was echoed by a senior Federal Bureau of Investigation agent involved with the case, who said: "The Marines perceived a target-practicing shot as a threat to their safety. . . . From that point, their training and instincts took over to neutralize a threat." The Justice Department ultimately paid $1.9 million to the Hernandez family to settle a wrongful death lawsuit.

> *The danger to civilians would not be limited to the border itself. Federal law allows [Border Patrol] checkpoints as far as 100 miles inland from the border or shoreline.*

The new proposals to use troops for border patrol work would greatly multiply the dangers revealed by the Hernandez incident. Unlike the soldiers deployed for the drug war, the troops on border patrol duty would be given arrest authority and allowed to directly engage civilians. And the danger to civilians would not be limited to the border itself. Federal law allows the Border Patrol to set up checkpoints as far as 100 miles inland from the border or shoreline.

It is true that U.S. soldiers have successfully guarded other countries' borders for years. But patrolling the demilitarized zone on the Korean peninsula is a far cry from enforcing U.S. immigration laws in Texas or Maine. The American borders with Canada and Mexico, two peaceful neighbors with whom Americans trade heavily, are rife with ambiguous situations and opportunities for conflict. Having soldiers enforce the immigration laws is not wise, it is not necessary, and it is not legal. If more immigration and border enforcement personnel are needed, they should be hired. Border security can be provided without the dangerous innovation of militarized borders. . . .

> *Patrolling the demilitarized zone on the Korean peninsula is a far cry from enforcing U.S. immigration laws in Texas or Maine.*

Before policymakers embrace proposals that will radically restructure the role of the American military, the dangerous implications of such a move must be carefully considered. Those dangers are not limited to collateral damage to civilians from combat-trained soldiers; they include threats to our open, participatory, republican institutions.

Will There Be Accountability?

"The blue wall of silence" is the popular term for a pattern of collusion and coverup that can often be found among police officers seeking to shield lawless violence and corruption in the ranks. [According to civil rights analyst David Rudofsky,] it denotes "an unwritten rule and custom that police will not testify against a fellow officer and that police are expected to help in any cover-up of illegal action." The blue wall of silence frustrates citizens and elected officials who are investigating possible abuses of power. Civilian authorities have developed institutions, such as internal affairs boards, that are designed to overcome that wall, but those institutions work only imperfectly, and cover-ups persist.

However much the code of silence obstructs the search for truth in cases of police abuse or negligence, the problem is likely to be far worse if policymakers expand and normalize the use of military policing. People trying to ascertain exactly what happened when citizens are killed or seriously injured by soldiers engaged in police actions on the home front are likely to run into a "green wall of silence" that will be even more impenetrable than the culture of secrecy in domestic police agencies. The prospect of lawless and unaccountable military units patrolling America should concern people across the political spectrum.

> *If more immigration and border enforcement personnel are needed, they should be hired.*

Consider, for example, the military's response to the previously mentioned Esequiel Hernandez incident, in which an American high school student was killed by a Marine Corps anti-drug patrol. The Pentagon and other federal agencies repeatedly stonewalled the local civilian investigators, according to Rep. Lamar Smith (R-TX), who conducted a congressional oversight inquiry into the circumstances surrounding the slaying. Two days after the incident, the soldiers involved in the shooting were abruptly transferred from the Texas border to Camp Pendleton, California, which obviously hampered the investigation of the incident. Rep. Smith's report notes that "the Marines were treated much differently from most potential suspects in homicide cases, and as a result they benefited from ample opportunities to coordinate and memorize their stories before being subjected to professional law enforcement interrogation." Moreover,

> During their criminal investigation, the Texas Rangers and District Attorney Valadez found it difficult to obtain necessary information, documents and testimony from the Marines, JTF-6 [Joint Task Force Six, the multiservice military command responsible for counterdrug operations within the United States] and the Border Patrol. The federal agencies failed to provide evidence in response to simple requests, so the District Attorney served subpoenas. The Defense Department responded to those subpoenas by asserting federal immunity.

Rep. Smith's investigation concluded that the Defense Department, along with the Justice Department, operated so as to "obstruct and impede state criminal law enforcement in the Hernandez case.". . .

Should use of soldiers to fight the domestic war on terror be expanded, the compelling public interest in government transparency will run up against a powerful legal barrier preventing disclosure of the facts when citizens are killed or injured. That barrier is the so-called state secrets privilege, [outlined in the 1952 *United States v. Reynolds* decision,] which allows federal agencies to shield information from civil or criminal courts when "compulsion of the evidence will expose military matters which, in the interest of national security, should not be divulged." Courts accord "utmost deference" to executive assertions of privilege on national security grounds. The judge will generally not examine the documents sought, to ensure that they in fact contain military secrets, lest too much judicial inquiry into the claim of privilege "force disclosure of the thing the privilege was meant to protect, [per the *Reynolds* decision]." If through a narrow review, a court satisfies itself that military secrets are at issue, "even the most compelling necessity [on the part of the litigant] cannot overcome the claim of privilege."

> *Border security can be provided without the dangerous innovation of militarized borders.*

There is no parallel claim of "public safety privilege" or the like protecting police methods and tactics from disclosure in cases involving civilian police personnel. That helps to keep the police accountable to the people. In contrast, the more policymakers turn to, and rely on, military personnel to fight crime domestically, the harder it will be for innocent injured parties to attain redress in the courts. . . .

What Should Be Done: Demilitarize the War on Drugs

For more than 20 years the federal government has steadily ramped up the militarization of the war on drugs. In 1986 President [Ronald] Reagan signed a National Security Decision Directive that declared the drug trade a "national security threat."

Congress, in a series of statutory revisions passed in the 1980s, made the war on drugs a bona fide war, with the Pentagon a central player in the struggle. Though those statutory provisions are commonly referred to as the "drug war exceptions" to the Posse Comitatus Act, they do not grant soldiers arrest authority. However, the provisions do encourage the Pentagon's involvement in surveillance and drug interdiction near the national borders. . . .

The loopholes for military participation in the drug war have done damage enough. By putting heavily armed and inappropriately trained Marines on the U.S.-Mexican border, the "drug war" exceptions to the Posse Comitatus Act led inexorably to the death of Esequiel Hernandez. And by encouraging the transfer of military ordnance to civilian peace officers, the drug war exceptions have encouraged a dangerous culture of paramilitarism in police departments.

Given this record, the Pentagon's move to divert resources from drug interdiction is a step in the right direction. But that policy change is not nearly enough. Instead of a sub rosa effort to limit Pentagon involvement in the war on drugs, Congress should repeal the "drug war exceptions" to the Posse Comitatus Act. American military personnel should be focusing on Al Qaeda operatives who are plotting mass murder, not marijuana smugglers. . . .

Weapons of Mass Destruction

There are limited areas in which military expertise, equipment, and even personnel can help to secure Americans from terrorist threats—and where such assistance does not present the kind of dangers the Posse Comitatus Act is designed to prevent.

For example, there are 32 Civil Support Teams currently operational in the United States, tasked with responding to suspected chemical, biological, or radiological attacks. The teams are not combat units; rather, they consist of full-time National Guardsmen specially trained in analyzing and responding to threats involving weapons of mass destruction (WMD). The Civil Support Teams operate under the command of their respective state governors, but they can be placed under federal command, if necessary. They bring special expertise and capabilities not normally available to civilian first responders—such as high-tech mobile laboratories that can allow the teams' WMD experts to analyze suspected chemical or biological agents on-site to determine whether the suspected threat is genuine. If it is, the teams advise civilian authorities on the likely consequences and preferred courses of action. Congress has authorized the creation of 23 additional teams.

> **"** The Posse Comitatus Act of 1878 . . . makes it a criminal offense to use U.S. military personnel as a police force. **"**

The Civil Support Teams are a good example of how military resources can be deployed effectively and appropriately to improve homeland security. Regrettably, most other proposed domestic uses of American military post-9/11 have not met that standard. Public officials, most of them outside the uniformed services, have uncritically accepted the notion that because the military has been so spectacularly effective at its appointed task of waging war, it can be equally effective providing security on the home front. That notion is as simplistic as it is dangerous.

No Panacea

The U.S. military is the most effective fighting force in human history; it is so effective, in fact, that some federal officials have come to see it as a panacea for domestic security problems posed by the terrorist threat. But on the home front, there are many tasks for which the military is ill suited, and for which its deployment would be profoundly unwise.

The soldier's mission, as soldiers often phrase it, is "killing people and breaking things." In contrast, police officers, ideally, are trained to operate in an environment where constitutional rights apply and to use force only as a last resort. Accordingly, Americans going back at least to the Boston Massacre of 1770 have understood the importance of keeping the military out of domestic law enforcement. That understanding is reflected in the Posse Comitatus Act of 1878, which makes it a criminal offense to use U.S. military personnel as a police force.

In the more than two years since the terror attacks of September 11, 2001, however, there has been a slowly building chorus of calls to amend or weaken the Posse Comitatus Act and give the U.S. military a hands-on role in homeland security. Prominent figures in Congress and the Bush administration have complained that legal barriers to domestic militarization tie their hands in protecting the American people. Of course, where appropriate, we *want* constitutional and statutory constraints to "tie the hands" of the authorities in their pursuit of domestic security. Safety and security are not the only ends of government—liberty is our highest political end. The Posse Comitatus Act is, unfortunately, a weak and porous barrier to military involvement in domestic law enforcement, but it is designed to protect both our liberty and our safety.

Changed circumstances after September 11 provide no compelling reason to weaken the statute further. Moreover, the disturbing history of Army involvement in domestic affairs strongly cautions against giving the military a freer hand at home.

7

U.S. Ports and Cargo Are Not Secure

Stephen E. Flynn

Stephen E. Flynn is a senior fellow in the National Security Studies Program at the Council on Foreign Relations, and director of the council's Independent Task Force on Homeland Security Initiatives. A former commander in the U.S. Coast Guard, Flynn is the author of America the Vulnerable: How Our Government Is Failing to Protect Us from Terrorism.

Millions of tons of freight crosses U.S. borders every day, 90 percent of it arriving in $40' \times 8' \times 8'$ containers that are alarmingly vulnerable to exploitation by terrorists and criminals. The U.S. agencies responsible for inspecting and authorizing passage of these shipments have enough personnel and equipment to examine only 1 to 2 percent of that cargo, and current security measures are insufficient to prevent terrorists from using a container as a vehicle for high explosives or chemical weapons, or even the less likely biological weapon or nuclear device. Beyond the destruction and loss of life a cargo-borne terrorist attack could cause, such an incident would likely halt containerized cargo shipments and bring the transportation industry, and the economy, to their knees. Security safeguards must be implemented now, including strict controls over the legitimacy of container contents at the point of origin, foolproof ways of verifying that container integrity has not been violated in transit, and cooperation between U.S. trade partners.

Stephen E. Flynn, statement to the U.S. Senate Committee on Governmental Affairs, Washington, DC, March 20, 2003.

[In 2002] I joined with former senators Warren Rudman and Gary Hart in preparing our report, "America: Still Unprepared—Still In Danger." We observed that [on September 11, 2001] nineteen men wielding box-cutters forced the United States to do to itself what no adversary could ever accomplish: a successful blockade of the U.S. economy. If a surprise terrorist attack were to happen tomorrow involving the sea, rail, or truck transportation systems that carry millions of tons of trade to the United States each day, the response would likely be the same—a self-imposed global embargo. Based on that analysis, we identified as second of the six critical mandates that deserve the nation's immediate attention: "Make trade security a global priority, the system for moving goods affordably and reliably around the world is ripe for exploitation and vulnerable to mass disruption by terrorists.". . .

The Shortcomings of the Intermodal Container

U.S. prosperity—and much of its power—relies on its ready access to global markets. Both the scale and pace at which goods move between markets has exploded in recent years thanks in no small part to the invention and proliferation of the intermodal container. These ubiquitous boxes—most come in the 40' × 8' × 8' size—have transformed the transfer of cargo from a truck, train, and ship into the transportation equivalent of connecting Lego blocks. The result has been to increasingly diminish the role of distance for a supplier or a consumer as a constraint in the world marketplace. Ninety percent of the world's freight now moves in a container. Companies like Wal-Mart and General Motors move up to 30 tons of merchandise or parts across the vast Pacific Ocean from Asia to the West Coast for about $1600. The transatlantic trip runs just over $1000—which makes the postage stamp seem a bit overpriced.

> *The system that underpins the . . . movement of global freight . . . was built without credible safeguards.*

But the system that underpins the incredibly efficient, reliable, and affordable movement of global freight has one glaring shortcoming in the post-9-11 world—it was built without credible safeguards to prevent it from being exploited or targeted by terrorists and criminals. Prior to September 11, 2001, virtually anyone in the world could arrange with an international shipper or carrier to have an empty intermodal container delivered to their home or workplace. They then could load it with tons of material, declare in only the most general terms what the contents were, "seal" it with a 50-cent lead tag, and send it on its way to any city and town in the United States. The job of transportation providers was to move the box as expeditiously as possible. Exercising any care to ensure that the integrity of a container's contents was not compromised may have been a commercial practice, but it was not a requirement.

The responsibility for making sure that goods loaded in a box were legitimate and authorized was shouldered almost exclusively by the importing jurisdiction. But as the volume of containerized cargo grew exponentially, the number of agents assigned to police that cargo stayed flat or even declined among most trading nations. The rule of thumb in the inspection business is that it takes five agents three hours to conduct a thorough physical examination of a single full intermodal container. [In 2002] nearly 20 million containers washed across America's borders via a ship, train, and truck. Frontline agencies had only enough inspectors and equipment to examine between 1–2 percent of that cargo.

> *For would-be terrorists, the global intermodal carrier system . . . satisfies the age-old criteria of opportunity and motive.*

Thus, for would-be terrorists, the global intermodal container system that is responsible for moving the overwhelming majority of the world's freight satisfies the age-old criteria of opportunity and motive. "Opportunity" flows from (1) the almost complete absence of any security oversight in the loading and transporting of a box from its point of origin to its final destination, and (2) the fact that growing volume and velocity at which containers move around the planet create a daunting "needle-in-the-haystack" problem for inspectors. "Motive" is derived from the role that the container now plays in underpinning global supply chains and the likely response by the U.S. government to an attack involving a container. Based on statements by the key officials at U.S. Customs, the Transportation Security Administration, the U.S. Coast Guard, and the Department of Transportation, should a container be used as a "poor man's missile," the shipment of all containerized cargo into our ports and across our borders would be halted. As a consequence, a modest investment by a terrorist could yield billions of dollars in losses to the U.S. economy by shutting down—even temporarily—the system that moves "just-in-time" shipments of parts and goods.

Social and Economic Consequences

Given the current state of container security, it is hard to imagine how a post-event lock-down on container shipments could be either prevented or short-lived. One thing we should have learned from the 9-11 attacks involving passenger airliners, the follow-on anthrax attacks, and even [the 2002] Washington sniper spree is that terrorist incidents pose a special challenge for public officials. In the case of most disasters, the reaction by the general public is almost always to assume the event is an isolated one. Even if the post-mortem provides evidence of a systemic vulnerability, it often takes a good deal of effort to mobilize a public policy response to redress it. But just the opposite happens in the event of a terrorist attack—especially one involving catastrophic consequences. When these attacks take place, the assumption by the general public is almost always to presume a general vulnerability unless there is proof to the contrary. Government officials have to confront head-on this loss of public confidence by marshalling evidence that they have a credible means to manage the risk highlighted by the terrorist incident. In the interim as recent events have shown, people will refuse to fly, open their mail, or even leave their homes.

If a terrorist were to use a container as a weapon-delivery device, the easiest choice would be high-explosives such as those used in the attack on the Murrah Federal Building in Oklahoma City. Some form of chemical weapon, perhaps even involving hazardous materials, is another likely scenario. A bio-weapon is a less attractive choice for a terrorist because of the challenge of dispersing the agent in a sufficiently concentrated form beyond the area where the explosive devise goes off. A "dirty bomb" is the more likely threat vs. a nuclear weapon, but all these scenarios are conceivable since the choice of a weapon would not be constrained by any security measures currently in place in our seaports or within the intermodal transportation industry.

> *" Should a container be used as a 'poor man's missile,' the shipment of all containerized cargo into our ports and across our borders would be halted. "*

This is why a terrorist attack involving a cargo container could cause such profound economic disruption. An incident triggered by even a conventional weapon going off in a box could result in a substantial loss of life. In the immediate aftermath, the general public will want reassurance that one of the many other thousands of containers arriving on any given day will not pose a similar risk. The President of the United States, the Secretary of Homeland Security, and other keys officials responsible for the security of the nation would have to stand before a traumatized and likely skeptical American people and outline the measures they have in place to prevent another such attack. In the absence of a convincing security framework to manage the risk of another incident, the public would likely insist that all containerized cargo be stopped until adequate safeguards are in place. Even with the most focused effort, constructing that framework from scratch could take months— even years. Yet, within three weeks, the entire worldwide intermodal transportation industry would effectively be brought to its knees—as would much of the freight movements that make up international trade. . . .

Strategies for Reducing the Risk

At its heart, risk management presumes that there is a credible means to (1) target and safely examine and isolate containers that pose a potential threat, and (2) identify legitimate cargo that can be facilitated without subjecting it to an examination. The alternative to risk management is to conduct random inspections or to subject every cargo container to the same inspection regime. Risk management is the better of these two approaches for both economic and security reasons. The economic rationale is straightforward. Enforcement resources will always be finite and delays to legitimate commerce generate real costs.

Less obvious is the security rationale for risk management. There is some deterrent value to conducting periodic random inspections. However, since over 90 percent of shipments are perfectly legitimate and belong to several hundred large importers, relying on random inspections translates into spending the bulk of the time and energy on examining those containers by the most frequent users of containerized cargo who are most likely to be perfectly clean.

> *The choice of a weapon would not be constrained by any security measures currently in place in our seaports or within the intermodal transportation industry.*

Examining 100 percent of all containers is not only wasteful, but it violates an age-old axiom in the security field that if "you have to look at everything, you will see nothing." Skilled inspectors look for anomalies and invest their finite time and attention on that which arouses their concern. This is because they know that capable criminals and terrorists often try to blend into the normal flow of commerce, but they invariably get some things wrong because they are not real market actors. But, an aggressive inspection regime that introduces substantial delays and causes serious disruption to the commercial environment can actually undermine an enforcement officer's means to conduct anomaly detection. Accordingly, allowing low risk cargo to move as efficiently as possible through the intermodal transportation system has the salutary security effect of creating a more coherent backdrop against which aberrant behavior can be more readily identified.

Deciding which cargo container rates facilitated treatment, in turn, requires satisfying two criteria. First, an inspector must have a basis for believing that when the originator loaded the container, it was filled only with goods that are legitimate and authorized. Second, once the container is on the move through the global intermodal transportation system, an inspector must have the means to be confident that somewhere along the way it has not been intercepted and compromised. If he cannot point to a reliable basis for assuming these two criteria are satisfied, in the face of a heightened terrorist threat alert, he must assume that the container poses a risk and target it for examination.

Prior to the most recent post-9/11 initiatives to enhance container security, the means for concluding that a shipment was legitimate at its point of origin was based strictly on an evaluation of the requisite documentation. If there were no discrepancies in the paperwork and a shipper had a good compliance track record, their shipments were automatically cleared for entry. But, the requirements surrounding the documentation for these "trusted shippers," charitably put, were nominal. For instance, shippers involved in consolidating freight were not required to itemize the contents or identify the originator or the final consignee for their individual shipments. The cargo manifest would simply declare the container had "Freight All Kind" (F.A.K.) or "General Merchandise." The logic behind taking this approach was straightforward when the primary inspection mandate was to collect customs duties. The Internal Revenue Service does pretty much the same thing for individual taxpayers. The presumption is as long as a company maintains appropriate in-house records, the data presented up front can be kept to the bare minimum. Compliance can be enforced by conducting audits.

> *There are a number of relatively straightforward ways to break into a container, including removing the door hinges, without disturbing the seal.*

Inspectors intent on confirming that the integrity of a container has not been violated on its way to its final destination, rely primarily on a numbered-seal that is passed through the pad-eyes on the container's two doors. As long as the number on the seal matches the cargo manifest and there are no obvious signs of tampering, the container's contents are assumed to be undisturbed. This remains the case today even though front-line enforcement agents have known for some time that there are a number of relatively straightforward ways to break into a container, including removing the door hinges, without disturbing the seal.

The inherent limits of relying on these enforcement tools to confront the terrorist threat were starkly demonstrated in the June 2002 prototyping of what has become the "Operation Safe Commerce" initiative. This prototype involved tracking a container of automotive light bulbs from a manufacturing facility in Slovakia to a distribution center in Hillsborough, N.H. A global positioning system (GPS) antenna was placed on the door of the container and was connected to a car-battery inside the container which served as its power source via a wire that passed through the door's gasket. For anyone who was not forewarned that this was a sanctioned experiment, this equipment should have looked a bit scary. Yet, the container ultimately crossed through five international jurisdictions without any customs official ever raising a question. When the container made the trip on its final leg from Montreal to Hillsborough, N.H., the driver took 12 hours to make what should have been a 3½ hour trip, having made several unauthorized stops along the way.

> *Even the most trusted shippers currently possess little to no capacity to monitor what happened to their freight when it is in the hands of their transportation providers.*

The OSC prototype highlighted a core reality of modern global logistics—even the most trusted shippers currently possess little to no capacity to monitor what happened to their freight when it is in the hands of their transportation providers. As long as it arrives within the contracted time frame, they have had no incentive to do so. Accordingly, any effort to advance container security must have as its ultimate objective the development of the means to assure the integrity of a shipment from its starting point through its final destination. . . .

Support from Trade Partners Is Essential

Developing enhanced container security standards will require actively enlisting the support of U.S. trade partners. The inclusion of transportation security as an agenda item in the 2002 G8 Summit and the most recent OPEC [Organization of Petroleum Exporting Countries] meeting in Thailand are commendable in this regard. I am particularly enthusiastic about an effort underway in northern New England to partner with the Canadian government and the Ports of Halifax and Montreal to undertake a follow-on Operation Safe Commerce initiative. Canada is our largest trade partner and is vested in ensuring the cross-border shipment of goods is not interrupted by serious security breeches that originate outside North America as well as within the continent.

Ultimately, this agenda will require ongoing support by senior officials and policy makers in the Department of State, the Department of Commerce, the Department of Treasury, and the U.S. Trade Representative as well as others involved in promoting U.S. interest overseas. It will also require a substantially larger investment in federal resources than have been made available to date. At the end of the day, container security is about constructing the means to sustain global trade in the context of the new post-9-11 security environment. We cannot afford to be penny-wise and pound foolish in advancing this vital agenda.

8

New Federal Regulations Are Improving Port and Cargo Security

Asa Hutchinson

Asa Hutchinson is undersecretary of the Border and Transportation Security (BTS) directorate within the U.S. Department of Homeland Security. His oversight includes the Bureau of Customs and Border Protection.

Since September 11, 2001, the federal government has implemented three new initiatives designed to secure U.S. ports and cargo. First, the Container Security Initiative (CSI) targets U.S.-bound cargo at foreign ports. CSI identifies high-risk cargo containers based on intelligence profiles, prescreens these containers using sophisticated technology such as radiation detectors, and encourages the replacement of existing containers with more secure, tamper-evident models. An important feature of CSI is the so-called twenty-four-hour rule, which requires the presentation of complete cargo manifestos twenty-four hours prior to loading a container on a vessel. The second initiative, the Customs-Trade Partnership Against Terrorism (C-TPAT), targets the entire supply chain—importers, customs brokers, shippers, and truckers. Companies that improve their own supply-chain security, tightening procedures and inspections to meet C-TPAT standards, receive expedited processing at U.S. borders. The third initiative, Operation Safe Commerce (OSC), is a public/private partnership formed to

Asa Hutchinson, statement to the U.S. Senate Committee on Governmental Affairs, Washington, DC, March 20, 2003.

research and test new technologies to safeguard commercial shipments against both terrorist attack and illegal immigration.

On March 1, 2003, the initiatives [discussed below] became Department of Homeland Security initiatives as the U.S. Customs merged with the Border Patrol and the immigration and agriculture inspection programs to form the Bureau of Customs and Border Protection, or BCBP. . . . BCBP is within the Department of Homeland Security's BTS Directorate.

As Secretary [Tom] Ridge has oft stated, our primary objective here at the Department is to prevent terrorism. At BTS, and specifically within the Bureau of Customs and Border Protection, our priority mission is preventing terrorists and terrorist weapons from entering the United States. That extraordinarily important mission means improving security at our physical borders and ports of entry, but it also means extending our zone of security beyond our physical borders. Indeed, the initiatives I am going to discuss . . . are designed to push our zone of security outward so that American borders are the last line of defense, not the first line of defense against the international terrorist threat. These initiatives—like all BTS Smart Border Initiatives—are designed, to improve security without stifling the flow of legitimate trade. In fact, many of these initiatives promote the more efficient movement of trade. Securing trade and facilitating trade are two of the main goals of the BTS Directorate. . . .

Container Security Initiative

Ocean-going sea containers represent the most important artery of global commerce—some 48 million full sea cargo containers move between the world's major seaports each year, and nearly 50 percent of all U.S. imports (by value) arrive via sea containers. That means nearly 6 million cargo containers arrive at U.S. seaports annually.

Because of the sheer volume of sea container traffic and the opportunities it presents for terrorists, containerized shipping is uniquely vulnerable to terrorist attack. Most experts believe that a terrorist attack using a container as a weapon or as a means to smuggle a terrorist weapon, possibly a weapon of mass destruction, is likely. If terrorists used a sea container to conceal a weapon of mass destruction and detonated it on arrival at a port, the impact on global trade and the global economy could be immediate and devastating—all nations would be affected.

The purpose of the Container Security Initiative, CSI, is to prevent and deter terrorists from using cargo containers to conceal terrorist weapons, including potentially nuclear weapons or radiological materials. Under CSI, which is the first program of its kind, we are identifying high-risk cargo containers and partnering with other governments to pre-screen those containers at foreign ports, before they are shipped to our ports.

> *[New] initiatives . . . push our zone of security outward so that American borders are the last line of defense, not the first line of defense against the international terrorist threat.*

The four core elements of CSI are:
- *First*, identifying "high-risk" containers. These are any containers that pose a potential risk for terrorism; i.e., that may contain—based on intelligence and risk-targeting principles—terrorist weapons, or even terrorists. We are using a structure called the Automated Targeting System (ATS), a sophisticated rules-based system, capable of sorting and processing vast quantities of information very rapidly to identify the "high-risk" containers.
- *Second*, pre-screening the "high risk" containers at the foreign CSI port before they are shipped to the U.S.
- *Third*, using technology to pre-screen the high-risk containers, so that it can be done rapidly without materially slowing down the movement of trade. This includes both radiation detectors and large-scale x-ray-type machines in order to detect potential terrorist weapons.
- *Fourth*, using smarter, "tamper-evident" containers—containers that indicate to BCBP officers at the port of arrival whether they have been tampered with after a security screening.

Under CSI, we have deployed and continue to deploy small teams of BCBP personnel to the foreign ports, of nations that are partners in the CSI initiative. These U.S. personnel target containers using computers that are connected to our Automated Targeting System (ATS) system here in the United States. Our host nation customs partners add information useful to the targeting process, using their own systems. Pooling our information and data results in better targeting decisions.

The next step is that the host nation's customs officers inspect the containers identified as posing a risk, using nonintrusive inspection (NII) and radiation detection equipment. The NII equipment generates x-ray and gamma ray images, which U.S. and host nation officers study for anomalies that could indicate the presence of terrorist weapons, including nuclear or radiological materials. In the event that an anomaly is detected through the NII or radiation detection equipment, the host nation's customs officers conduct a physical inspection of the contents of the container. U.S. Customs and Border Protection officers observe this entire process to make sure security protocols are followed.

> *Under CSI . . . we are identifying high-risk cargo containers and partnering with other governments to pre-screen those containers at foreign ports.*

CSI adds substantial security to containerized shipping without slowing down the flow of legitimate trade. Containers that have been pre-screened and sealed under CSI will not ordinarily need to be inspected again by U.S. Customs and Border Protection when they arrive at United States seaports. Currently, every container identified as high risk is being screened on arrival to the United States. With CSI, it will usually be unnecessary to do this screening here, if it has been done— "there"—at a CSI port.

CSI Implementation, Phases I and II

The Customs Service developed the CSI initiative in the last two months of 2001, and Commissioner [Robert C.] Bonner announced CSI in January, 2002. Since then, CSI has generated exceptional participation and support.

The goal for the first phase of CSI was to implement the program at as many of the top 20 foreign container ports—in terms of volume of cargo containers shipped to United States seaports—as possible, and as soon as possible. Those ports were the logical place to start CSI, because the top 20 alone account for nearly 70 percent, over two-thirds, of all cargo containers arriving at U.S. seaports. The top twenty ports include: Hong Kong, Shanghai, Singapore, Kaohsiung, Rotterdam, Pusan, Bremerhaven, Tokyo, Genoa, Yantian, Antwerp, Nagoya, Le Havre, Hamburg, La Spezia, Felixstowe, Algeciras, Kobe, Yokohama, and Laem Chabang.

> *CSI adds substantial security to containerized shipping without slowing down the flow of legitimate trade.*

Within one year of the announcement of CSI, 18 of the top 20 ports agreed to participate in CSI. CSI has been implemented and is operational in Le Havre, France; Rotterdam, the Netherlands; Antwerp, Belgium; Bremerhaven and Hamburg, Germany; and in Singapore, the largest container transshipment port in the world. . . .

BCBP is in the process of formulating the second phase of CSI. Under CSI Phase 2, the CSI program will be implemented at other foreign ports that ship a significant volume of cargo to the United States, and that have the infrastructure and technology in place to support the program. Sweden and Malaysia have already signed CSI agreements for this phase. [As of March 2003] a total of 14 countries have agreed to implement CSI.

The 24-Hour Rule

Because CSI involves getting and using information about containers before those containers leave foreign ports, the advance transmission of complete and accurate vessel cargo manifest information to BCBP is essential to its success. Advance transmission of that information is also essential to overall successful targeting of high-risk cargo containers from any port, regardless of whether that port is part of CSI, because the better the information and the sooner we have it, the more effective and efficient U.S. Customs and Border Protection can be in identifying high-risk cargo and screening that cargo for terrorist weapons, including nuclear and radiological material.

A final advance manifest regulation relating to oceangoing

cargo was issued on October 31, 2002, requiring the presentation of accurate, complete manifest information 24 hours prior to loading of a container on board a vessel at the foreign port. Under that regulation, vague descriptions of cargo, such as "FAK" (Freight All Kinds), are no longer acceptable. On February 2, 2003, a strategy was begun to ensure compliance with the so-called "24-hour rule," following a 60-day grace period to permit the trade to adjust its business practices. BCBP is continuing that strategy. The compliance strategy has involved issuing "no load" orders and denying permits to discharge containers in the event of non-compliance.

> *Under [the 24-hour rule], vague descriptions of cargo, such as 'FAK' (Freight All Kinds), are no longer acceptable.*

In the first month of enforcement, BCBP issued approximately 150 "no load" orders, but the trade is working very hard to comply and we are seeing significant compliance with many aspects of the rule.

If high-risk containers are identified after they have set sail for the United States, BCBP makes a determination on their level and source of risk. Depending on that assessment, BCBP has protocols in place for working with a variety of agencies, such as the Coast Guard to take appropriate next steps. For example, when a determination is made that cargo should not reach U.S. shores, BCBP works with the Coast Guard to ensure that the cargo is screened and examined, including the possibility of conducting examinations at sea.

Customs-Trade Partnership Against Terrorism

The Customs-Trade Partnership Against Terrorism, C-TPAT—developed and started by the Customs Service in January 2002—is an initiative designed to further reduce the risk that terrorist weapons could be concealed in cargo shipped to the United States. It does this by substantially improving security along the entire supply chain, not just at foreign seaports. By partnering with the trade community—U.S. importers, customs brokers, carriers, shippers, and others—we can better protect the entire supply chain against potential exploitation by terrorists or terrorist weapons.

Under C-TPAT, companies sign an agreement with BCBP to conduct a comprehensive self-assessment of their supply chain security and to improve that security—from foreign loading docks to the U.S. border and seaports—using C-TPAT security guidelines. These guidelines were developed with a large amount of input from the trade community, and include such items as procedural security, physical security, personnel security, education and training, access control, manifest procedures, and conveyance security.

Those companies that meet C-TPAT security standards receive expedited processing through our land border crossings, through our seaports, and through our international airports. This partnership enables us to spend less time on lower-risk cargo, so that we can focus our resources where they are needed most—on higher-risk cargo. It is a program through which businesses win, government wins, and, most importantly, the American people win.

> *[Under Operation Safe Commerce,] specific supply chains along particular trade routes are identified; then every aspect of the supply chain, from packaging to delivery, is analyzed for vulnerabilities.*

Over 2,000 companies—2,060 as of March 13, 2003—are participating in C-TPAT and have signed agreements with BCBP to improve the security of their supply chains. Members of C-TPAT include 60 of the top 100 importers and 32 of the 50 largest ocean carriers. Collectively, C-TPAT companies represent 90 percent of the containerized sea cargo entering the United States, and about 40 percent of all imports by value.

Currently, importers, carriers, brokers, freight forwarders, and non–vessel operating common carriers are eligible to apply for participation in C-TPAT. In January 2003, we also began accepting applications from domestic marine port authorities and terminal operators, who are already encouraged to participate in the U.S. Coast Guard Navigation and Vessel Inspection Circular (NVIC) program for waterfront facilities. We have plans to expand C-TPAT to foreign manufacturers and shippers as well.

Finally, to ensure the consistency of guidelines provided to operators of marine ports and terminals, BCBP and the Coast Guard have worked closely to ensure that the Coast Guard's (NVIC) programs for waterfront facilities are consistent with C-TPAT guidelines for Ports and Terminal environments.

Operation Safe Commerce

Operation Safe Commerce (OSC) is a public/private partnership being implemented by the TSA [Transportation Security Administration] dedicated to finding methods and technologies to protect commercial shipments from threats of terrorist attack, illegal immigration, and other contraband, while minimizing the economic impact upon the vital transportation system.

OSC involves developing and testing technology and systems to improve container security, consistent with the principles and security practices of ongoing security programs, such as CSI and C-TPAT. Specific supply chains along particular trade routes are identified; then every aspect of the supply chain, from packaging to delivery, is analyzed for vulnerabilities. Based on this analysis, plans will be developed to improve security throughout the entire supply chain, and potential solutions will be tested in an actual operating environment.

Specifically, OSC is addressing three key components to secure supply chain management. They are: (1) demonstrating what is needed to ensure that parties associated with commercial shipping exert reasonable care and due diligence in properly packing, securing, and manifesting the contents of a shipment of goods in a container; (2) demonstrating various methods to ensure that information and documentation associated with these shipments is complete, accurate, and secure from unauthorized access—this may entail transmitting information in a secure electronic format; and (3) testing supply chain security procedures and practices in order to determine the impact of these procedures when combined with the implementation of enhanced manifest data elements and container sealing procedures (including effective intrusion detection), to determine the most effective method to reduce the susceptibility of a shipment in transit in an international or domestic supply chain to illicit interference.

OSC is to be carried out using the three major U.S. container load centers: Seattle/Tacoma, New York/New Jersey, and Los Angeles/Long Beach. Seventy percent of U.S. container movement originates or terminates at these centers. . . . OSC's Executive Steering Committee, which is co-chaired by the Deputy Commissioner of BCBP and the Associate Deputy Secretary of the Department of Transportation, is responsible for managing OSC. The Transportation Security Administration, the Coast Guard, the State Department, the Commerce Department, the Justice Department, and the Homeland Security Council also have individual representatives on the Steering Committee.

Practical Enhancements

CSI and the 24-Hour Rule provide a mechanism for the U.S. Government to appropriately scrutinize the international movement of marine containers coming to the USA. The cooperative efforts of the federal government and the regulated parties in C-TPAT and OSC allow realistic, practical, business-oriented enhancements to that scrutiny. This provides more assurance of a secure international trade network, allowing BTS to deliver on securing and facilitating trade.

9

New Technology Is Improving Port and Cargo Security

Amitabh Avasthi

Amitabh Avasthi is a science writer for Technology Review, *a magazine of the Massachusetts Institute of Technology in Cambridge.*

U.S. and foreign agencies have intensified efforts to manually inspect high-risk cargo containers, but only have enough resources to inspect 5 percent of the 6 million containers that arrive in the United States annually. The best response to this vulnerability lies in sophisticated technology, relying first on electronic seals affixed to each container to automatically track its path and detect intrusions. Also in development are "smart" containers, manufactured with multiple sensors that recognize an unacceptable condition and report it, along with a container's location and identity. Recognizing the biggest threat, a nuclear or radioactive bomb, is also possible through the use of gamma ray detectors capable of revealing the shape of contents emitting radiation and ruling out harmless items such as medical supplies. These technologies are expensive, but not as costly as failing to detect and prevent a catastrophic terrorist attack.

The cargo container—that ubiquitous truck-sized box that carries goods around the world—could be the ultimate poor man's missile. Each year more than 48 million loaded cargo containers move between the world's seaports. But of the six

Amitabh Avasthi, "Containing Terror: Electronic Seals and Tracking Efforts Boost Cargo Security," *Technology Review*, vol. 106, September 2003, pp. 24–25. Copyright © 2003 by the Association of Alumni and Alumnae of MIT. Reproduced by permission.

million that arrive in the U.S., only 5 percent have their contents visually inspected or x-rayed, opening the possibility that terrorists could use them to smuggle in nuclear material, explosives, or even themselves. Many of the world's ports are joining a U.S.-led effort to manually inspect containers considered high risk; but at the same time, a host of technologies are being readied to plug this security hole.

Electronic Seals

It's a big job that starts with small electronic seals. [In the spring of 2003] Savi Technology of Sunnyvale, CA, and 65 technology companies and shipping industry partners concluded the first test of a new class of electronic seals that both track containers and detect intrusions. Affixed to a container's main latch, the seal has two functions. First, it serves as a radio frequency identification tag, allowing a container's movements to be recorded automatically when it passes tag readers on loading cranes and port gates or in distribution facilities. That's a technology already common in military containers, and it was recently used during the Iraq war.

But the new seals go a step farther, detecting break-ins. Opening the container breaks a magnetic field surrounding the seal; this event, and the time it took place, are recorded on a memory chip. The next time a breached container passes a tag reader, an intrusion alarm is automatically triggered, flagging the container for inspection.

> *A host of technologies are being readied to plug this security hole. It's a big job that starts with small electronic seals.*

The test was successful enough that several thousand seals have already been deployed to various government agencies and major shippers. According to Lani Fritts, a vice president of business development for Savi, the same consortium of 65 companies has now begun a second global field test that will ultimately involve 5,000 containers fitted with the electronic seals. What's more, the infrastructure being set up by the consortium will communicate automatically with government agencies like U.S. Customs and Border Protection.

Some of the containers in this new batch are being equipped for continuous communication; Savi is working with Qualcomm of San Diego, CA, to connect the seals with transponders that can communicate with satellite tracking systems, sending alerts in real time no matter where a container is located—on the high seas, at port, or bumping along on a truck chassis or railcar. Because continuous real-time communication is more expensive—how much more is not yet clear—the initial tests involve high-risk cargo like hazardous materials, or high-value cargo such as pharmaceuticals.

"Smart Containers"

The cargo industry's next goal is more ambitious: to introduce the world's first "smart containers," with multiple sensors manufactured into them. Savi is working with CIMC of Shenzen, China, the world's largest cargo container manufacturer, to design and develop the first prototypes by the end of [2003.] . . . These next-generation containers could be in commercial production [in 2004.]

> *A smart container . . . can transmit a tamper alert either via the Internet or by setting off a light or sound alarm. . . . Additional sensors could detect chemicals, radiation, and the residue of explosives.*

A smart container made from scratch will do much more than detect if its main seal has been breached. For example, if an intruder tries to cut or drill through its sides, light and motion sensors inside can communicate with the seal, which can transmit a tamper alert either via the Internet or by setting off a light or sound alarm. In the future, additional sensors could detect chemicals, radiation, and the residue of explosives. Such a container would have "a 'mayday' capability, in which it can recognize an unacceptable condition and report its identity, location, and condition," says Michael Wolfe, principal of the North River Consulting Group of North Marshfield, MA, which advises government and industry on security technologies.

But even the smartest containers may still need inspections: an inspector who learns that a container has been breached might need to find out what has been placed inside. Today's technologies, however, are inadequate for detecting the biggest threat: a nuclear bomb or radioactive "dirty bomb."

Gamma Ray Detectors

One possible solution: a gamma ray detector with an additional imaging component that reveals the shape of the materials emitting radiation. That's what a group led by Richard Lanza, a nuclear engineer at MIT, has prototyped. It's an array of small detectors that collect gamma rays and produce a fine energy spectrum that gets processed into a faint image of the radiating object.

This allows inspectors to identify innocent materials that give off small amounts of radiation—like certain medical supplies or objects made from granite—without wasting time on manual inspections. Prototypes of the detectors are currently being tested at the Lawrence Livermore National Laboratory in Livermore, CA.

Deployment will depend on the outcome of these tests, but the MIT device is part of an ambitious vision for the future of nuclear-explosives detection, says Richard Wagner, a physicist at Los Alamos National Laboratory who is helping evaluate new detection technologies for the federal government. "Eventually we hope to deploy hundreds of thousands of detectors" everywhere from seaports to highway border crossings, he says. Such a grand scheme might cost $10 billion; but the cost of detecting a nuclear bomb, clearly, is much cheaper than the cost of letting one through.

Organizations to Contact

The editors have compiled the following list of organizations concerned with the issues debated in this book. The descriptions are derived from materials provided by the organizations. All have publications or information available for interested readers. The list was compiled on the date of publication of the present volume; the information provided here may change. Be aware that many organizations take several weeks or longer to respond to inquiries, so allow as much time as possible.

American Civil Liberties Union (ACLU)
125 Broad St., 18th Fl., New York, NY 10004-2400
(212) 549-2500
e-mail: aclu@aclu.org • Web site: www.aclu.org

The ACLU is a national organization that works to defend Americans' civil rights guaranteed by the U.S. Constitution, arguing that measures to protect national security should not compromise fundamental civil liberties. It publishes and distributes policy statements, pamphlets, and press releases such as "In Defense of Freedom in a Time of Crisis" and "National ID Cards: 5 Reasons Why They Should Be Rejected."

American Enterprise Institute (AEI)
1150 Seventeenth St. NW, Washington, DC 20036
(202) 862-580 • fax: (202) 862-7177
Web site: www.aei.org

The American Enterprise Institute for Public Policy Research is a scholarly research institute that is dedicated to preserving limited government, private enterprise, and a strong foreign policy and national defense. AEI publishes books, including *Study of Revenge: The First World Trade Center Attack and Saddam Hussein's War Against America*. Articles about terrorism and September 11 can be found in its magazine *American Enterprise* and on its Web site.

The Brookings Institution
1775 Massachusetts Ave. NW, Washington, DC 20036
(202) 797-6000 • fax: (202) 797-6004
e-mail: brookinfo@brook.edu • Web site: www.brookings.org

The institution, founded in 1927, is a think tank that conducts research and education in foreign policy, economics, government, and the social sciences. In 2001 it began America's Response to Terrorism, a project that provides briefings and analysis to the public and that is featured on its Web site. Other publications include the quarterly *Brookings Review*, periodic *Policy Briefs*, and books, including *Terrorism and U.S. Foreign Policy*.

CATO Institute
1000 Massachusetts Ave. NW, Washington, DC 2001-5403
(202) 842-0200 • fax: (202) 842-3490
e-mail: cato@cato.org • Web site: www.cato.org

The institute is a nonpartisan public policy research foundation dedicated to limiting the role of government and protecting individual liberties. It publishes the quarterly magazine *Regulation*, the bimonthly *Cato Policy Report*, and numerous policy papers and articles. Works on border issues include the transcript "Panel Discussion on Immigration and Border Security" and the foreign policy briefing "The New Homeland Security Apparatus: Impeding the Fight Against Agile Terrorists."

Center for Defense Information
1779 Massachusetts Ave. NW, Suite 615, Washington, DC 20036
(202) 332-0600 • fax: (202) 462-4559
e-mail: info@cdi.org • Web site: www.cdi.org

The Center for Defense Information is a nonpartisan, nonprofit organization that researches all aspects of global security. It seeks to educate the public and policy makers about issues such as weapons systems, security policy, and defense budgeting. It publishes the weekly *Defense Monitor*, the issue brief "National Missile Defense: What Does It All Mean?" and the studies "Homeland Security: A Competitive Strategies Approach" and "Reforging the Sword."

Center for Immigration Studies
1522 K St. NW, Suite 820, Washington, DC 20005-1202
(202) 466-8185 • fax: (202) 466-8076
e-mail: center@cis.org • Web site: www.cis.org

The Center for Immigration Studies is the nation's only think tank dedicated to research and analysis of the economic, social, and demographic impacts of immigration on the United States. An independent, nonpartisan, nonprofit research organization founded in 1985, the center aims to expand public support for an immigration policy that is both pro-immigrant and low-immigration. Among its publications are the background papers "The USA PATRIOT Act of 2001: A Summary of the Anti-Terrorism Law's Immigration-Related Provisions" and "America's Identity Crisis: Document Fraud Is Pervasive and Pernicious."

Federal Aviation Administration (FAA)
800 Independence Ave. SW, Washington, DC 20591
(800) 322-7873 • fax: (202) 267-3484
Web site: www.faa.gov

The Federal Aviation Administration is the component of the U.S. Department of Transportation whose primary responsibility is the safety of civil aviation. The FAA's major functions include regulating civil aviation to promote safety and fulfill the requirements of national defense. Among its publications are *Technology Against Terrorism; Air Piracy, Airport Security, and International Terrorism: Winning the War Against Hijackers;* and *Security Tips for Air Travelers.*

National Security Agency
9800 Savage Rd., Ft. Meade, MD 20755-6248
(301) 688-6524
Web site: www.nsa.gov

The National Security Agency coordinates, directs, and performs activities, such as designing cipher systems, which protect American information systems and produce foreign intelligence information. It is the largest employer of mathematicians in the United States and also hires the nation's best code makers and code breakers. Speeches, briefings, and reports are available at its Web site.

U.S. Department of State, Counterterrorism Office
Office of Public Affairs, Room 2507
U.S. Department of State
2201 C St. NW, Washington, DC 20520
(202) 647-4000
e-mail: secretary@state.gov • Web site: www.state.gov/s/ct

The office works to develop and implement American counterterrorism strategies and to improve cooperation with foreign governments. Articles and speeches by government officials are available at its Web site.

U.S. Immigration and Customs Enforcement
U.S. Department of Homeland Security, Washington, DC 20528
(202) 282-8000
Web site: www.ice.gov

With the establishment of the Department of Homeland Security (DHS), the investigative and intelligence resources of the U.S. Customs Service, the Immigration and Naturalization Service, the Federal Protective Service, and the Federal Air Marshals Service were merged and reconstituted into Immigration and Customs Enforcement (ICE), the DHS's largest investigative bureau. Its diverse responsibilities include investigation and control of narcotics, weapons, and all other contraband smuggling; investigating exports of dual-use equipment that may threaten national security; deportation of aliens under immigration law; and deterring and defeating hostile acts targeting U.S. air carriers and airports. An archive of news releases, fact sheets, and congressional testimony, updated daily, is available at its Web site.

Bibliography

Books

Peter Andreas and Thomas J. Biersteker	*The Rebordering of North America: Integration and Exclusion in a New Security Context.* New York: Routledge, 2003.
Leo C. Bollinger and Geoffrey R. Stone, eds.	*Eternally Vigilant: Free Speech in the Modern Era.* Chicago: University of Chicago Press, 2002.
Steven Brill	*After: How America Confronted the September 12 Era.* New York: Simon & Schuster, 2003.
Kurt M. Campbell and Michèle A. Flournoy	*To Prevail: An American Strategy for the Campaign Against Terrorism.* Washington, DC: CSIS Press, 2001.
Lynn E. Davis	*Organizing for Homeland Security.* Santa Monica, CA: Rand, 2002.
James X. Dempsey and David Cole	*Terrorism and the Constitution: Sacrificing Civil Liberties in the Name of National Security.* Washington, DC: First Amendment Foundation, 2002.
Craig Eisendrath, ed.	*National Insecurity: U.S. Intelligence After the Cold War.* Philadelphia: Temple University Press, 2000.
Steven Emerson	*American Jihad: The Terrorists Living Among Us.* New York: Free Press, 2002.
Ted Gottfried	*Homeland Security Versus Constitutional Rights.* Brookfield, CT: Twenty-First Century, 2003.
Philip H. Melanson	*Secrecy Wars: National Security, Privacy, and the Public's Right to Know.* Washington, DC: Brassey's, 2001.
National Research Council	*Making the Nation Safer: The Role of Science and Technology in Countering Terrorism.* Washington, DC: National Academies Press, 2002.
Michael E. O'Hanlon et al.	*Protecting the American Homeland: A Preliminary Analysis.* Washington, DC: Brookings Institution, 2002.
John V. Parachini, Lynn E. Davis, and Timothy Liston	*Homeland Security: A Compendium of Public and Private Organizations' Policy Recommendations.* Santa Monica, CA: Rand, 2003.
Daniel Pipes	*Militant Islam Reaches America.* New York: W.W. Norton, 2002.
William Rivers Pitt	*The Greatest Sedition Is Silence: Four Fears in America.* London: Pluto, 2003.

| Marcus J. Ranum | *The Myth of Homeland Security.* Hoboken, NJ: John Wiley and Sons, 2003. |

| Daniel Ratner and Mark Ratner | *Nanotechnology and Homeland Security: New Weapons for New Wars.* Saddle River, NJ: Prentice-Hall/PTR, 2003. |

| Bruce Schneier | *Beyond Fear: Thinking Sensibly About Security in an Uncertain World.* New York: Copernicus, 2003. |

Periodicals

| Robert Block and Gary Fields | "Is Military Creeping into Domestic Law Enforcement?" *Wall Street Journal*, March 9, 2004. |

| Steven Brill | "The Biggest Hole in the Net: One Day Soon, America May Be Rocked by a Suicide Bomber. We Have No System to Deal with That Eventuality. Why the Debate over a National ID Card Is Long Overdue," *Newsweek*, December 30, 2002. |

| Charlotte Bunch | "Whose Security?" *Nation*, September 23, 2002. |

| Robert Cottrol | "Homeland Security: Restoring Civic Virtue," *American Enterprise*, January/February 2003. |

| Ivo H. Daalder and I.M. Destler | "Behind America's Front Lines: Organizing to Proect the Homeland," *Brookings Review*, Summer 2002. |

| *Economist* | "A Hole in the Middle: Homeland Security," September 7, 2002. |

| Michael Hirsh | "How Much Safer Are We? Despite Progress, America Remains Vulnerable Around the Edges," *Newsweek*, September 15, 2003. |

| Donald Kerwin | "The Catholic Tradition on Migrants Amid Heightened Security Concerns," *Origins*, August 28, 2003. |

| Charles Krauthammer | "The Case for Profiling," *Time*, March 18, 2002. |

| James Andrew Lewis | "Three Reforms to Make America More Secure—Intelligence, Government Organization, Law, and Technology Must Change to Build U.S. Security," *World & I*, October 2002. |

| Nelson Lund | "The Conservative Case Against Racial Profiling in the War Against Terrorism," *Albany Law Review*, Winter 2002. |

| Timothy Lynch | "More Surveillance Equals Less Liberty: Patriot Act Reduces Privacy, Undercuts Judicial Review," *The Hill*, September 10, 2003. |

| Eric R. Taylor | "The New Homeland Security Apparatus: Where the Phoenix Came Home to Roost," *CovertAction Quarterly*, Fall 2003. |

| Philip Zelikow | "The Transformation of National Security," *National Interest*, Spring 2003. |

Index